A How-To-Do-It Manual for Assessing, Allocating and Reorganizing Collections, Resources and Facilities

Library Space Planning

Ruth A. Fraley and Carol Lee Anderson

LIBRARY SPACE PLANNING

A How-To-Do-It Manual for Assessing, Allocating and Reorganizing Collections, Resources and Facilities

RUTH A. FRALEY
CAROL LEE ANDERSON

*HOW-TO-DO-IT MANUALS
FOR LIBRARIES*
Number 5

Series Editor: Bill Katz

NEAL-SCHUMAN PUBLISHERS, INC.
New York, London   1990

Published by Neal-Schuman Publishers, Inc.
23 Leonard Street
New York, NY 10013

Printed and bound in the United States of America

Photographs
Special thanks to Jerome Yavarkovsky, Director of the New York State Library,
and to James Corsaro, Associate Librarian, Manuscripts and Special Collections,
New York State Library, for locating and making available the photographs of
the New York State Library reproduced on page 16.

Library of Congress Cataloging-in-Publication Data

Fraley, Ruth A.
    Library space planning.

    (How to do it manuals for libraries ; no. 5)
    Includes bibliographical references.
    1. Libraries—Space utilization.   2. Library
fittings and supplies.   3. Library materials—
Storage.   4. Library buildings.   5. Library planning.
6. Library moving.   I. Anderson, Carol Lee.
II. Title.   III. Series.
Z679.55.F73   1985   022'.3   89-13311
ISBN 1-55570-040-3

DEDICATED TO
BILL AND STEPHEN

CONTENTS

SERIES EDITOR'S PREFACE

As with the successful first edition, this second edition of *Library Space Planning* is a practical guide for the librarian faced with the problems associated with making more room for books, people, and services. Whether the scenario includes moving into new quarters or reorganizing existing space, the difficulties are as insidious as they are innumerable. Here Ruth Fraley and Carol Anderson lead the weary librarian to sensible, easy-to-follow solutions.

The authors begin by pointing out that "space planning has become a frequent activity in the library. . . . Some libraries, often the larger ones, have committed time and resources to developing space plans or programs." True, but most of them apply to individual situations, and rarely—if only due to lack of funding—to medium and smaller libraries. Even the largest has difficulty because of the specific nature of the plans. This is where the present manual is of great assistance: the authors offer a matrix that can be adopted for almost any conceivable space problem.

All the steps involved in best exploiting space are explained, from communicating with novices about what to do when additional shelving is needed to how to keep the public happy in the middle of shifting the periodicals from the basement to the first floor. And it is done in such a way that one does not have to be an architect or a plumber to understand what is going on. Even the individual who has difficulties hooking up a VCR will have no problem with either the organization or the prose in this guide.

Organization is another strong point. The set of directions begins where it should, with an introduction to the goals and objectives. What should one look for when a space crisis arises. What steps should be taken, which steps should be avoided, and how can one gain the cooperation of staff and users who must suffer through the shifts. With that out of the way, the authors take us forward into the land of collecting. And here is one of the great services of their guidance. See, for example, the section on measuring the collection and how to tell how much space to give to what and, more important, how to evaluate what is needed and what goes where.

The success of the work owes much to the authors' first-hand experience with the problems. They know libraries as well as any librarians around, and understand what is likely to be a first-class headache. They can then pass the aspirin. This is nowhere better demonstrated than in the chapter on alternatives for the collection space dilemma. The authors clearly explain compact shelving, outlining the advantages and disadvantages. Microform and enclosed storage options are also considered and, again, a clear account is given. It's the details that count. How many librarians have found tips on such a variety of solutions as fore-edge shelving and flat shelving, moving the existing shelving, or double-shelving books?

Having just put up a two-by-two tool shed, this writer can fully appreciate a chapter that dares to consider in depth how one assesses the building, from floor plans to windows and back again. Jumping ahead a bit, one then finds a chapter on "Starting the Project"—after all the planning is completed. It contains invaluable advice on layouts and timetables.

The chapter devoted to library operations during the move offers practical advice on how to run things when half the library is in chaos. Those who doubt the authors' workaday experience need only turn to one compelling sentence: "All moves share four common elements: noise, dirt, security problems, and altered traffic patterns." Thus speak veterans of the trenches. They go on, as they do on every page, to tell the reader how to stay alive during the working bombardment.

In the final section, on moving and wrap-up, Fraley and Anderson note, "Moving a library is like painting a room." It is this type of comparison that brings it all home to the novice who may never have shifted a book from point x to point y, but has undoubtedly had some experience with a paint brush.

Earlier, the authors say that some work exists in this field. They are being unduly modest. Even a casual glance at *Library Literature* reveals the lack of material on the minor art and major headache of moving. It has been left to the authors to come up with the advanced guide. They are the scouts who cheerfully take us on a perilous journey. If one contrives to end sane, it is because of their affable, reasonable belief in common sense and in the active intelligence of the reader.

A word, too, about the new edition. For those who cherished the first, now take up the second. There is even more to learn, more areas covered (such as automation and its implications), and more diagrams to enhance this eminently usable guide.

Bill Katz

PREFACE

In 1983, we wrote the first draft of the first edition of *Library Space Planning* on an electric typewriter, which was then state-of-the-art equipment for the home office. Subsequent drafts were written on an Osborne I microcomputer with a five inch wide screen and 64K capacity. Disks were single-sided and held about 12 pages of text each, if we left room to edit the text. While working with the Osborne, we had the opportunity to upgrade the machine for double-sided, double-density disks and to upgrade the RAM to 96K—a grand adventure, to be sure.

As we began work on this edition just a few years later, we were working on hard drives with modems to transfer files, and with monitors on both machines at least 12″ wide. And if there is yet another edition, we suspect that we will be working out of our home offices with laptops containing 40mg internal hard drives, with digitizing equipment to input the edits we will be faxing back and forth. In the span of a few years, the popularization of reasonably priced technology has completely changed writing.

Katie Blake's remarks describe the magnitude of the technological change: "In 1970, the idea of a computer on every desk was laughable. By 1987, it had become the norm. In 1980, it seemed ridiculous to think of a laptop, portable microcomputer. By 1987, they were almost mandatory for the traveling businessperson."[1] When we wrote the first edition in 1983, environmentally sound room-to-house mainframes or minis and outlets and phone line chaseways for circulation system terminals, OCLC, or online searching terminals constituted the major library technology space considerations. A few far-seeing innovators were providing public access pc's or public access terminals for online searching, and special libraries often included dumb terminals for the company computer. Obviously, the technology has advanced a great deal and will continue to advance, driving many new applications and therefore altering space requirements to house the equipment and its evolving uses.

As we work on this new, large-format edition, the most exciting space-saving implication of technology *per se* is the proliferation of information stored in CD-ROM format. Use of CD-ROM technology will come to replace some print materials, microforms, card files, and some online services because it is affordable and easily understood by the end user.

Technology for the sake of technology is rarely affordable or desirable. While it can be an efficient tool for accomplishing the goals of serving library clientele and managing operations more efficiently, the demands on existing structures, arrangements, and furnishings are constantly changing. And these exponential changes will continue. David P. Norton and Ronald L. Evans encapsulate the enormity of these changes in "Keeping Pace with Technology."[2] They describe the evolution of pc use: Phase 1 is the Transformation of Tasks, changing the way people work and making individuals more productive; Phase 2 is the Transformation of Process, making business more productive, changing the economics of the business, and changing the business organization; Phase 3 is the Transformation of Business, changing the way the business works and creating breakthrough business. Library organizations are still in Norton and Evans' Phase 1, although a very few have entered Phase 2. All three phases have a significant impact on the ways that we assess, allocate and utilize space.

REFERENCES

1. Katie Blake, "The Electronic Book" *Library Hi Tech*, 6 (Issue 21, 1988): 7.
2. David P. Norton and Ronald L. Evans, "Leadership: Keeping Pace with Technology" *PC Computing*, 2 (January 1989): 206.

INTRODUCTION

Library Space Planning was written to provide a systematic method and practical guide for successful re-use of library space within existing facilities. It is intended to guide managers of all types of libraries through stages ranging from the planning of initial building assessments through the implementation of a library space reorganization.

The majority of books and articles that discuss library moves, reorganizations, and space allocation assume that an ideal situation exists. However, planning time, new buildings, adequate funds, architects, and knowledgeable outside consultants are not always available due to fiscal or other constraints. Occasionally the project is very small, with minimal, if any, fiscal resources to commit to anything other than actual construction. Sometimes the project is to be undertaken without additional resources, but must be funded from the operating budget. Space reorganization decisions are often made without adequate information, or time, and as a reaction to pressure to "do something" about a situation that has become untenable. *Library Space Planning* offers assistance to the librarian faced with a space dilemma and meager resources to summon.

We suspect that the report of the Massachusetts Board of Library Commissioners issued in 1987 is indicative of library space in other states and regions and the results are applicable to all types of libraries. "Survey results indicated that a large percentage of library facilities are over 20 years old and that many of these have never had a renovation or addition since the date of construction. . . . A total of 81 of these structures [represented on the survey] were not originally constructed as public library facilities. The original use ranges from carriage house, school, supermarket, or church to private residences."[1]

The information explosion, automation, financial constraints, and simply running out of room have combined to place considerable additional pressure on already stretched library facilities. Older library buildings designed at the turn of the century and the sealed buildings of the 1960's do not meet any basic criteria for energy efficiency, ability to handle automated systems, or room for materials of varying formats. More often than not, today's librarian must cope with a situation in which the space available fails to match the space needed in either form or function.

Librarians must plan carefully and use every square foot of assignable space in a manner which will help them fulfill their library's mission. *Library Space Planning* will guide the library space planner through the entire process. Chapter One discusses organizational goals in relation to the need to act on the space situation and concludes with advice for creating a space plan. The detailed directions in Chapters Two, Three and Four provide information for systematically gathering data about an individual library in order to draw up the local space plan or "plan of action." The collection and the collection housing are examined first; the information gathered can be used when reviewing the suggested alternatives to a collection-growth space dilemma.

The raw data are completed by compilation and examination of information about the library facility, its furnishings, and equipment, as explained in Chapter Four; all of the information gathered is then used to draw up a plan or program for addressing a library's space needs. Chapter Five provides guidelines and a methodology for establishing a library-space reorganization budget.

Chapter six presents guidelines for a vital aspect of library reorganization: effective and well-planned communication before, during, and after the project. Another important part of a space plan occurs in the last planning steps: the details to be covered before a move or reorganization occurs. Chapter Seven provides examples and guidelines for setting up timetables, drawing the required layouts, and selecting the move method; it also details other preparations necessary before actually beginning to realign the staff, collection, equipment, and furnishings. Chapters Eight and Nine examine the actual process of moving a library into a new configuration. These two chapters cover maintaining library services during a move, the traps encountered during a move, and tips for avoiding these traps.

Library Space Planning ends as a move is completed. The mechanism is in place for gathering information for an ongoing evaluation of space utilization and the inevitable rearrangement of facilities to meet evolving demands on library operations.

REFERENCE

1. Massachusetts Board of Library Commissioners, *Long Range Program, 1987-1991* (Boston: ERIC Document 279339, 1987): 20.

1 PREPARING A SPACE PLAN

Since the first edition of this book, space planning has become a frequent activity in the library world, and the growth of technology as a resource as well as tool for library operations has been exponential and significant. Some libraries, often the larger ones, have committed time and resources to developing space plans or programs. Several of these programs have been published and are cited in the Bibliography. Two of the more recent ERIC documents are examples of these publications. The University of Idaho at Moscow issued its "Library Facility Study" in August, 1986 (ED277 376, 188 pages).

The report was prepared by the university's Department of Facility Planning, Joanne Reece, Director. It is the result of a two-year space needs analysis of the University of Idaho Library and focuses on the three primary space requirement elements: users, collection components, and library staff and support services. The "Report of the Task Force on Facilities, Space, and Equipment" documents an investigation conducted to determine how the University of California, Santa Barbara Library could best use its facilities, space, and equipment to meet the needs of users; to provide a safe, comfortable workplace for staff; and to house and protect its collections. (ED 297 730, 166 pages).[1]

There are four key situations in library operations that will precipitate space reorganization:

> lack of collection-growth space
> lack of space for people
> a change in direction or mission of the organization or community served by the library
> and introduction of new services.

All libraries—special, school, public, and academic—have to deal with at least one of these circumstances sometime. The situation may be predictable, identified as part of the long-range plans for the library or defined as part of a needs assessment process. While the situation often evolves from the introduction of technology into library operations, it may also appear without apparent warning, a product of several different factors. The first step in reorganizing any library is to identify the key problem or problems. In some situations—as, for example, when automation or technology is being introduced the primary problem can be easily identified. Accurate assessment of the problem guides the process of selecting space alternatives and provides a framework for decision making during reorganization.

Photographs courtesy of the New York State Library

REASONS FOR REORGANIZATION

COLLECTION GROWTH SPACE

When the terms "overcrowded library" or "library space problem" are used, the collection space problem is the one most easily envisioned. A collection growth space problem is just as serious but not as easily pictured. People can imagine books falling on the floor or stacked in boxes in the corridors. The imagery is real in more than a few libraries. People who visited the stacks at the New York State Library in the mid 1970's before its move to the new facility can probably remember the piles of books around the metal winding stairwells. There are many libraries with books stacked on windowsills, on top of shelves, and in the aisles.

Lack of collection-growth space is a problem long before it gets to be a crisis and the image becomes reality. Recognition of the problem in a timely manner and identification of alternative solutions before it reaches the crisis stage save labor and damage to materials. Solutions, discussed in Chapter Three, include a variety of creative shelving techniques, implementing zero collection growth, converting print materials to nonprint formats or using technology to replace in-house collections.

When viable alternatives have been investigated and considered in relation to the library operation, awkward and time-consuming activity can be avoided. The non-librarian, providing input as a member of the county board or school board or as a library trustee, may suggest another alternative: stop purchasing new materials. This is sometimes presented as a solution to two problems: space constraints and declining purchasing power.

In order to avoid well-intentioned but negative suggestions, the librarian must continually examine collection-growth space alternatives from a long-range perspective. An up-to-date space data file containing accurate information about the status of collection space requirements and a long-range space plan incorporating phased collection space alternatives can be effective tools in discussions with non-library people, especially those who control fiscal resources.

The collection space problem is not always obvious. One example is a small library that was created when a hotel was converted to a community college. The basic building configuration was an open space with columns at regular intervals. Since the building planners designed the library for an open access collection, the stacks were laid out around the columns with special-order, permanently installed shelving.

This was an attractive arrangement, but did not allow for the installation of more shelving as the collection grew, nor for the addition of any nonprint materials. Reshelving was always delayed, and many books were permanently housed on booktrucks. Once patrons learned the classification system, they spent a great deal of time circling the columns. In addition, there was no central monitoring point where a staff member could keep an eye on the activities behind the columns. Visitors assumed the library was poorly run because there were always booktrucks blocking the aisles and it was very difficult to follow the call number sequence.

ACCOMMODATING PEOPLE

The driving force for change in a library's space plan may be centered around people: the staff and/or users. This situation usually becomes evident after collection-growth space has been added, often at the expense of "people" space, or when there is no room for the introduction of a new service, such as public access personal computers or CD-ROM equipment, or when automation of library services is extensive enough to change not only job descriptions but de facto library operation.

Library Staff: Changes in job responsibilities and organizational structure, excessive staff turnover, difficult personalities, and poor productivity are library-staff issues that may be addressed, in part, by space reorganizations. Turnover is costly, diverting funds and staff energy from other library purposes. One way to reduce turnover is to improve the physical conditions and surroundings. Occasionally the solution can be simple: adding a row of lockers to provide a secure, private place for each staff member; painting; adding soundproof dividers; or moving workstations that have been located in one place for a long time. Many libraries have a proportionately large number of staff working at minimum wage or at the beginning level of clerical service. If staff members have to face poor working conditions in addition to low wages, a high turnover rate is not surprising.

One example of a space problem arising from staff considerations is the library whose director felt the public services staff were not being as productive as possible. His solution was to locate all workers where they were visible to him at all times. This department now has a high turnover rate, and regular confrontations take place between patrons and staff over office noises such as computer printers, ringing telephones, and business conversations.

Office-design factors generate staff problems when the design makes it impossible to work efficiently. Poorly designed work areas precipitate the re-evaluation of space utilization. One of the most problematic designs is the open office or open work area. We have been in enough offices where walls and soundproof dividers were constructed to revise open-space design to be convinced that open-space design fails more often than it succeeds. Staff reductions and scarce resources mandate maximum productivity from all workers. If staff productivity can be increased by putting up dividers and providing some privacy, then the dividers are necessary equipment.

In some libraries, the office design or arrangement has to change because a staff member must be isolated due to the nature of his or her responsibilities. Personnel duties and confidential discussions with patrons are two examples of situations requiring privacy. In other cases, productivity is enhanced by rearranging workstations so people are located near colleagues who help their work go more smoothly.

Office designs that delay the flow of materials or cause an increased number of steps to complete a task must be reworked. As work changes, so does the office design required to do the work; a small change in workflow can necessitate a change in the workspace arrangement. Invariably, a new office design will be required when the operations or functions are automated.

When staff positions are eliminated from the library, job descriptions have to be rewritten and the work flow modified to assure completion of the work. Assignment modification precipitates revised space allocations. The same is true for a staff increase, which often occurs when funding becomes available for a special project. Additional staff need a place to work, even if they are temporary employees.

The arrangement of work stations in relation to the patrons and the flow of library traffic also results in people-space allocation problems. If desks for the behind-the-scenes workers are located at a service point, misunderstandings with patrons occur. For example, few patrons will understand why a staff member who happens to be working near a photocopy machine is not the one who refills the paper tray.

Another example is the library that adds a community reception room where regularly scheduled group activities take place. If the route to this room is through the cataloging department, something will have to be changed so the staff can avoid constant interruptions from group traffic and security of materials can be arranged.

Automation of library functions generates changes in job responsibilities, which in turn affects space allocation. The two problems that have to be dealt with concern people and organizational change. The addition of microcomputers and fax machines, for example, not only requires redesigned work stations but new definitions of tasks and working relationships. Even basic automation will require some change. A word processor and printer, for example, use more space than a typewriter and require at least two more duplex outlets.

Library Users: Planning skill and a knowledge of library operations are important in defining the nature of user space needs, which must be considered in all of the space-planning steps, regardless of the key element identified. For example, user requirements for an online catalog are different from those of a traditional catalog, even though the key element in this reorganization would be the same—the automation of the catalog.

Lack of adequate seating space for patrons is a common problem. When the patrons rearrange furniture constantly, make service points inaccessible, and must constantly queue for service, they are communicating that the library mission has not been translated into an effective space utilization plan. Over the years, the available patron seating space is often eroded to such an extent that the total library operation is affected.

Inadequate seating may be a result of inappropriate seating. Perhaps an entire floor is devoted to lounge seating, even though patrons really need a quiet place for study. Problems arise in school libraries when a class is taught in the library at the same time other students are trying to study independently. The recalcitrant student sent to the library from the classroom requires a relatively isolated area away from the students doing research. A public library may discover that more users are at the library for story hours than job seeking services, or that the demand for small group meeting space has been translated into regular meetings at the referral tables. Academic and law libraries may discover that reference books are constantly being "borrowed" because there is not enough space on site to use the materials. Adding a CD-ROM station to an existing carrel will make user space inadequate. The workspace and characteristics of the carrel are lost, and the user will find conditions for using the equipment to be inadequate; often, there is no writing surface near the machine.

In some public libraries, the diversity of services has caused some available user space to be committed to one large room which can serve as a gathering place for the community; often another area or room has been created to allow public access to microcomputers and Compact Disc Read Only Memory (CD-ROM) readers. The availability of teleconferencing dictates a viewing room, or at least a video hook up in the community room. Special purpose rooms are fine, but if they have been created at the expense of user seating, there may be some problems to cope with.

Service ramifications of poor user space decisions are illustrated in the example of the small academic library where all service points were consolidated in response to complaints about the level of noise throughout the library. However, the space for the combined service points was not large enough to handle the operations; no one looked at the annual report of the previous year to determine the number of questions handled at each of the separate service points. The combined service point did reduce noise in one location of the library—a positive result. The negative result was apparent when over 100,000 transactions were handled in the same space that had handled under 10,000 transactions the previous year. Patrons were frustrated, and staff felt the pressure. The new service desk was placed between two columns, eliminating expansion space as well as the possibility of setting up separate stations. Had the decision makers used the annual report data, the number of transactions handled at the new service point would not have been such a surprise.

Noise is another problem forcing a space reconfiguration. The photocopy machines, microform readers, computer printers, conversations at the reference desk, circulation system printers, slamming doors, traffic patterns, buzzing security devices, video soundtracks, speaker systems for guest lecturers, cheers from the story hour, and the sounds and echoes that are a part of the architecture, influence the use of the library space and the user's perceptions of the library. Quiet reading and study space is becoming increasingly difficult to find in all types of libraries.

Budget cutbacks have resulted in a lack of funds for building maintenance and furniture repair. Reassignment of space is often mandated to best utilize remaining furniture or to accommodate items available from city, school district, company, or college "surplus." Lounge furniture wears out more quickly than other furnishings, but since replacement is usually based on what is available rather than what is most desirable, the result may be "new" furniture not suited to library needs.

A decision on user-space arrangements made during another era

DESIGN ALTERNATIVE #1

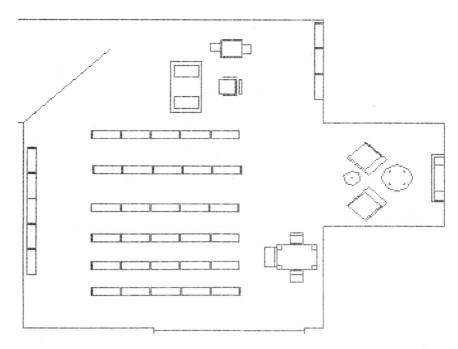

Figure 1. Overview of original layout shows lack of seating, poor visibility and wasted space.

FIGURES 1 AND 2

The original configuration for a small public library shown in Figures 1 and 2 included lounge furnishings in the alcove area. The fireplace, easy chairs, and low table created a casual atmosphere and seating for only two people.

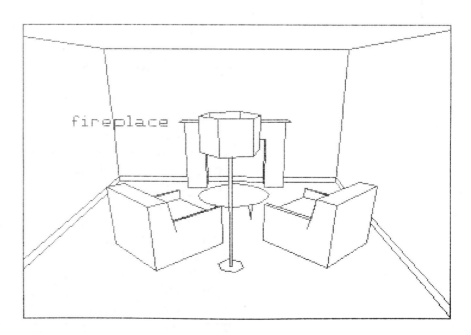

Figure 2. View of the alcove with lounge chairs.

is often not applicable to present needs. User space may have to be rearranged to meet fire codes or for regulations governing accessibility for the physically handicapped. A number of remodeling projects undertaken during the 1970s involved changes to improve access, including widening aisles and doorways, adding railings and ramps for stairs, and housing special equipment to reach and use materials.

INTRODUCTION OF NEW SERVICES

Each time a new service is introduced, it must be viewed from a space utilization perspective. If the planner—whether librarian, architect, or consultant—is unable to adequately anticipate the space ramifications of such new services as additional meeting rooms, on-site job or tax consulting, a reserve operation, public access computers or database searching, then the service might not work. The primary reason for this failure will be the improper allocation of library space.

A number of factors must be considered when planning new service space:

> the prospective clientele and their attributes
> the probable hours the service will be offered and most heavily used
> security for staff and equipment
> equipment and wiring requirements
> lighting requirements
> and the anticipated service load—a preschool story hour has different space needs from the fee based business reference or the intensive, research-assistance interview.

Adding public access CD-ROM ERIC searching, for example, is exciting to staff and users. However, planners will want to locate a spot not only with appropriate electrical outlets but also with minimal glare on the screen, space for a printer, if one is part of the unit, proximity to other CD-ROM databases, and space for the user to take notes near the machine. The location should be visible to a library staff member, whose presence may deter theft and damage as well as provide assistance as needed.

When space is committed to a new special service, remember that unless there is an addition to the library, the space must come from somewhere. Another service, collection, or work space must give way, and it will be changed. The ripple effect must be planned for.

ORGANIZATIONAL DIRECTION

A change in mission or organizational direction is one of the trickier problems to identify and to place in perspective. Major questions include:

What is the function of the library within the organization?
Whom does it serve?
What does the organization expect from the library?
What does the library expect to be able to provide to the organization?
Is the library's mission clearly understood by all?
Can the mission be translated into space allocation decisions?

Dale Montanelli discusses "organizing for space management." She talks about developing a master plan to achieve the goals a library administration has for the space available to the library. Her study provides a good framework for relating library objectives to available space. The data necessary for space management decisions, the use of space standards, and the "human factors in managing space" are also discussed.[2] The change in library goals for space utilization can drive a reorganization.

Organizational demands affect options about library space. When a finite amount of space is available, library space may be given up to a more politically powerful part of the organization. For instance, a new teacher may be assigned office space in the library; the county historian may have to be located in the library; the public library system headquarters may demand space in the library building; or a new academic department may be headquartered in the library.

Organizational space takeovers can occur if there is a perception that the space is not being used. Outsiders may not understand the need for materials conservation activities and corresponding space requirements, nor are work areas and processing areas easy to explain. Any empty seat is considered wasted space, and there seems to be a perverse rule in operation which permits empty seats whenever visitors or outside evaluators come into the library. Members of the organization who are not librarians will be confused about technical services and its functions; others will never understand why a librarian other than the head librarian needs an office.

FIGURES 3 AND 4

When a public access personal computer was added to available services, casual seating was eliminated as was the fireplace. The space planner used the occasion to shift the collection, adding a few sections of shelving and completely shifting the existing ranges in order to improve lighting and visibility from the service desk. Figures 3 and 4 show the revised layout and alcove arrangement.

DESIGN ALTERNATIVE #2

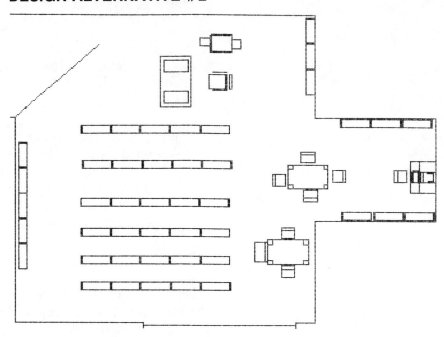

Figure 3. Overview shows additional user seating and new computer station.

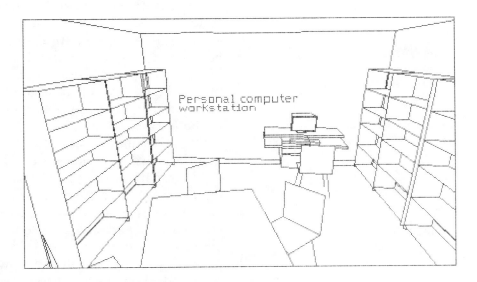

Figure 4. View of the alcove with new computer station.

When a library space reorganization project is mandated by a part of the organization other than the library, organizational problems are the key element. The objective precipitating the mandate and the impact on the library are major factors to consider in the library space planning process.

When inadequate library space is recognized as an issue, another problem often occurs: allocation of space inappropriate for library purposes. Because of organizational politics, it is sometimes necessary to accept whatever space is offered—whether it is the PTA that has generously offered its kitchen located three floors away from the school library, or the local business that has offered a full floor of space for storing library materials even though the floor is one step away from condemnation. The fact that the PTA plans to continue using the kitchen for hot-dog sales and the business has an energy-savings program whereby the building support systems are turned off in the evening at 5:00 p.m. are all factors to consider, not only in planning the use of the space, but also in negotiating for other space. Usually, if any space is offered, it must be used or lost and the loss will have political ramifications.

Demographics also influence the organization mission, although the change is often gradual and difficult to anticipate. Some ways in which demographics have influenced the use of library space include:

- An elementary school became a middle school; instead of kindergarten through grade six, students in grades five through eight are now in the building. Obviously, the collection needs changed. Space needs for instructional activities also changed.
- A college became a university and now awards graduate degrees in several new fields. Collections had to be expanded to serve in-depth research needs. Additional study carrels and seminar rooms are needed.
- A commuter college built dormitories and became a residential institution. The library had to adapt to the presence of a student body for 24 hours per day.
- A company moved several divisions of manufacturing and research from one city to another. Each library in the cities involved had to change collections and services.
- A new retirement community, replacing several multifamily units, was scheduled for construction two blocks from the library. The library space planner had to consider allowing for more meeting room space for special programming,

changing the collection emphasis, and perhaps modifying the children's and young adult programming.

THE LIBRARY SPACE PLANNER

Once the key elements of the library space environment have been identified, the planning process can start. The library space planner simultaneously investigates many aspects of the library and its environment. The demographic changes, institutional budgets, corporate reorganizations, automation, staff turnover, and new library services must be related to library space needs. Library space consultants can expedite each phase of the investigation and frequently identify alternatives beyond those visualized by the staff. Hiring consultants is a local decision contingent on funds, local expertise and staff time available, as well as the local political atmosphere. The literature about consultants should be reviewed before a final decision is made.[3] Whether or not a consultant is hired, one person from the library must be designated to serve as the "space planner," either developing plans internally or working with the library space consultant. This will take a considerable amount of that librarian's time, so his or her usual duties should be temporarily assigned to other personnel.

In a small library the library director often assumes the role of library space planner. In larger libraries, the director generally appoints a staff member to carry out this role. In our discussion throughout this book, the terms *space planner* and *project manager* are used interchangeably because once the plans and decisions are finalized, the space planner typically supervises the implementation of the project and indeed becomes a project manager.

The in-house person assigned the task of space planning must be able to cope with confusion, deliver projects and programs on target, examine and calculate space in minute detail, understand the relationship between parts of an operation and its whole, and think and react quickly in the context of a project goal. The library space planner also has to negotiate and work closely with contractors, maintenance crews, colleagues, consultants, and architects. If renovation or building is part of the project, the space planner will have to work with other professionals such as structural and construction engineers. All of these skills must be combined with the ability to visualize and to relate the vision and the library to the long-range goals of the organization. The project manager must be a shirtsleeve manager able to move a table or lift a box as needed, or show how it is done.

GATHERING INFORMATION FOR THE LIBRARY'S SPACE PLAN

After the key elements in the library space situation have been defined—whether by the head librarian, the library administrators working with the library space planner, or the library space consultant working with the staff and library-designated space planner—the primary goal of the project will fall into place. It may be more space for collections; more space for staff; revised use of existing space; space to be designed for a new service; or more space for users.

In order to identify and assess the options for meeting the goal, and to make the best decision for the local situation, the library space planner needs to gather relevant information and compile data. The information constitutes the space-data file and is then used to develop a library space plan. While the space data file contains the raw information, the space plan contains the proposed layouts and the projected use of the space stated, and illustrated, on long-term and short-term basis. The plan can be as complex as the local situation requires, but it must be dated and signed—and comprehensible to someone who has not been involved in its creation. As mentioned at the beginning of the chapter, the literature contains examples of library space plans or programs; the process is also discussed in detail for academic institutions in the second edition of Keyes Metcalf's work *Planning Academic and Research Library Buildings.*[4]

If planning for library facilities has been an ongoing process, the framework for implementing a space reconfiguration will be in place; the process for investigating local resources will exist; and it is possible that a library consultant as well as select members of the library staff will be familiar with measuring the facility. Unfortunately, full-blown planning is not always possible, particularly in medium to small libraries. In these cases, the space crisis should be viewed as an opportunity to establish local practices that will serve the library in the future.

THE SPACE DATA FILE

Space data file is a generic term. It may have several different formats, and the contents will vary from library to library—files, spreadsheets, notebooks, blueprints, surveys, floor plans, a box of papers—whatever meets local needs. Although the format is flexible, the information in the space data file is not. The result of the gathering process will be a detailed description of the library facilities use—past and present—and the basic information necessary for future planning. Each item must be dated and labeled as it is added to the file. Include the following information:

1. Institutional mission statement, goals and objectives, plus long-term projections or long-range plans. Institutions of higher education and school districts have been undergoing extensive long-range planning processes in order to efficiently address the economic constraints of the 1980's and 1990's. These documents identify the priorities for support to the organization and spell out its direction. Plans for corporations and professional firms are often found in annual reports or budgets. Each of these plans and statements will include an assessment of strengths and weaknesses, and most will identify resources required for future development.

2. Library mission statement, goals and objectives, and any long-term projections or long-range plans. Documentation about library operations should be complete and up-to-date. Lack of up-to-date information contributes to gaps between the stated and actual mission and between projected and actual space usage. Whatever the state of the documentation, it should be collected since it provides a starting point for assessing the library operations and planning space alternatives. Planning for space inevitably leads to planning for all library operations.

3. Institutional and library budget information; copies of the budgets, justifications, spending plans, and allocations. The budget of the organization is most informative when viewed as a whole, as opposed to examining only the section pertaining to the library. It can tell the space planner what percentage of the budget goes to the library; what percentage of institutional or municipal personnel are library personnel; and how this percentage has changed over the past few years. This information can indicate the possibility of additional support and its extent. The budget documents will also point out other pressing problems that may influence the availability of resources for the library. If there are other libraries within the organization, what is the difference in allocations among the libraries? Comparison of the differences over a couple of years will show clearly which departments or

areas received financial support and are therefore a priority. Note those programs or departments which received an increased percentage of the total available funding. Look for extenuating circumstances and one-time start-up costs. Was the telecommunications system converted to a new one? Was energy usage too high and a new monitoring system installed? At this stage, the library-space planner is seeking evidence that budgetary expenditures support organizational directions so that plans may be made for the library to fit into the larger picture.

4. Library space utilization reports and studies which might have been done in the past. These reports provide information about previous thinking and experiences; they will have to be updated and related to the present and projected goals of the library.

5. Photographs of past and current use of the library facilities. Photographs can save many hours of digging for obscure details. If the library floor held three fire trucks when it housed the fire department, or the building was once a factory, floor-loading questions are partially answered. Long-forgotten electrical connections, different types of furniture arrangements, and past utilization of space will also show up in photographs.

6. Collection and collection-housing measures and notes. This information is required in order to allocate shelving and to plan for future collection growth. The process is discussed at length in Chapter Two.

7. Equipment and furnishings inventory. Again, detailed information is required in order to devise a plan for using facilities. The process for gathering this information is discussed in Chapter Four.

8. Building blueprints for past arrangements, current arrangements, and space the library might acquire. These blueprints are used to experiment with possible arrangements and serve as the basis for the final space plan. Features of the building which are not evident on inspection may be revealed on the blueprints.

9. Institutional space inventory information, floor plans, and reports or studies about institutional space. This information is sometimes available only as a listing of square footage allocations.

10. Outline of present work flow and service points, accompanied by appropriate statistics. The outline should dem-

onstrate the progress of materials and information from ordering to receipt to service and housing. Find this information during the assessment process and draw it on one of the blueprints to give it graphic meaning. The appropriate statistics are from the previous annual report listing service, processing, and maintenance activities.

11. Budget information for the proposed project and for past projects. Proposals, bids, and specifications for earlier moves of the collections and arrangements of the space may be in the library's or institution's files.

DEVELOPING THE LIBRARY'S SPACE PLAN

The main goal or goals to be met have been defined and data gathered to support the process of revising the existing space plan or creating a new one. After the data and information are gathered, the space planner uses this information to identify options to address the identified needs and goals. For example, if the key element for the project is to introduce a new service, the data from measuring should yield information about any space in the library that will meet the requirements of the new service. It will also contain details about the present use of that space, enabling the planner to identify space or functions to be revised or eliminated in order to implement the new service. A space plan may contain phased implementation programs whereby the goal is attained by using the space in iterations. The initial information in a space plan contains a succinct summary of the activity to be implemented. The plan contains an outline of steps to be taken, resources required, and estimated time frame for implementation. Space plans are flexible documents that should be revised on a regular basis.

REFERENCES

1. "Library Facility Study" (University of Idaho at Moscow: ERIC Ed 277376, August 1986): 1-188.
   "Report of the Task Force on Facilities, Space, and Equipment" (University of California, Santa Barbara: ERIC Ed 297730, March 1986): 1-166.
2. Dale S. Montanelli, "Space Management for Libraries" *Illinois Libraries*, 69 (February 1987): 130-38.
3. Lester K. Smith, Editor, *Planning Library Buildings: From Decision to Design* (Chicago: American Library Association/Library Administration and Management Association, 1986). Papers from a LAMA Building and Equipment Section Preconference held in 1984. The work covers the building needs assessment process, development of building programs, and discussion on building design phases. Of particular interest are chapters by Gloria Novak, "Planning Teams for Library Buildings"; Margaret Beckman, "The Library Building Consultant and the Library Planning Team"; Joel G. Clemmer, "Decision-Making in Academic Library Building Planning"; and Nancy R. McAdams, "The Role and Selection of the Architect." Also see:
   Richard Boss, *Information Technology and Space Planning for Libraries and Information Centers* (Boston, G. K. Hall, 1987): 103-4.
   Warren J. Haas, "The Role of the Building Consultant" *College and Research Libraries*, 30 (July 1969): 365-68.
4. Philip D. Leighton and David A. Weber, *Planning Academic and Research Library Buildings*, 2nd Edition (Chicago: American Library Association, 1986): 70-81.

2 MEASURING THE COLLECTION

This chapter shows exactly how to measure and describe collections and the collection housing, two activities necessary for accurate and successful space planning. Measuring the existing collections and collection housing is most often done by library personnel. Sometimes outside or temporary help may be used. A consultant may design the measuring project or interpret its results.

The need for collection space is usually the key element in library space reorganizations. Since the collection uses the majority of assignable library space, its disposition determines the space allocations for all library operations. Through measuring the collection and the collection housing, the space planner gains an accurate and complete picture of the physical characteristics of these two components and has basic information to present to the consultant.

The space planning and space reorganization implementation process requires specific measurements necessary for identifying alternatives, making decisions about the space allocations, and planning the method and route of the move. All of this information becomes a significant part of the space data file. "The amount of work for repeat surveys can be reduced if capacity changes due to the addition or removal of stacks are recorded between space measurements. A complete stack capacity measure is necessary only once. Furthermore, a complete shelf space survey by actual measurement is required only once every several years, if statistical projections of shelf space are carried out during the interim."[1]

MEASURING COLLECTION HOUSING

SHELVING
Figure 1 illustrates the common configuration for a range of library shelving and labels the parts. A range is a series of connected shelving sections; it usually includes end panels. The frame or uprights support the shelves. Single-faced sections have shelves hung from only one side of the section supports. Double-faced sections have shelves attached to both sides of the support frames. Standard book shelving may be on one side of a double-faced section and display front shelving for current periodicals on the other side.

The number of shelf pieces, their color, and the manufacturer must be included in the space data file; these individual components comprise the raw materials needed to do the work when reconfiguring the stacks. The pieces which go into a shelving unit include shelf sides or supports, shelves, base plates, braces, support bars, and end panels. Metal library shelving usually has a right and a left side; if shelves are to be assembled, there must be a right and a left side to each section and a right and a left side to each shelf.

Ranges are usually tied together or braced for stability. Stability is sometimes provided by a supporting piece of metal anchored across the tops, perpendicular to the ranges. For brace-frame shelving, individual sections are braced by two metal support bars which form an "X" in the back of adjacent sections, distributing the weight. Metal support strips are also fastened to the walls and then to the end section of a range. *Include in the data gathering process all of the types of materials used for fastening and bracing.*

Shelving frames of all heights must be counted and noted. A standard section of library shelving is 90″ high, but some sections will be shorter or taller. The height of the section affects the linear footage of shelving available by defining the number of shelves that can be hung per section; standard library shelving usually has six to seven adjustable shelves per section depending on the material housed. Almost every library collection includes materials of varying heights. The arrangement for housing the quarto, folio, and undersized materials will affect the total number of shelves needed.

FIGURE 1

A common configuration for a range of library shelving.

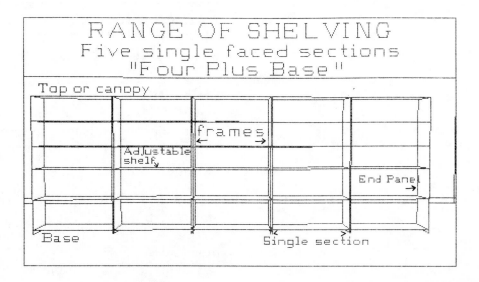

Standard library shelves are 36″ long. However, because of quirks in the physical facility, or to make a group of ranges end evenly, special shelves or sections are sometimes constructed. Shelf lengths of 30″, 39″, and 42″ are also found in older shelving installations. These variations and the use of nonstandard shelves mean that measuring the shelving should be done shelf by shelf. It is often not feasible to count the number of shelves and multiply by 3′ to determine the true number of linear shelf-feet available.

Shelves are generally either 8″, 9″, or 10″ deep. The varying shelf depths are used to house different types of materials. For example, an 8″ shelf loaded with scientific journals will bow or sag while a 10″ shelf will be just right for the load. *The shelf information in the space data file should list one figure for linear shelf-feet with subdivisions of quantity by shelf depth, color, and manufacturer.*

Since there as many special-purpose shelves and shelving sections as there are manufacturers, accuracy can be ensured by using a dual measure. Two teams should measure the shelving using the same forms, plans, and identifying features, but measure at different times. The process involves a close inspection of each shelf so that unique characteristics can be noted and recorded. For example, a shelf with special slots to hold sound recordings may have been preempted for books which will hide the slots; the dual measure will assure the space planner that this special feature is noted.

Collection housing, especially in a crowded library, will often include custom-designed or single-purpose racks or furniture. For example, paperback books are frequently housed on paperback racks or on window sills. There are many custom pieces of furniture for children's books, and often the back end of a table is pressed into use to house reference or legal material. If an item is used to house books, it should be considered part of the collection housing and measured and noted. Even if the intent is to stop using this equipment, it contributes to the linear footage in use for housing the library collection.

Use a floor plan of the existing stack layout as a master record to make notes and mark measuring progress through the collection. Start with a floor plan consisting of only wall, window, and door markings. Since teams will be working with copies of the same floor plan, it should show section and area numbers.

The library space planner working with the information will be able to compare forms from each team for the appropriate section on the floor plan and will be assured of an accurate picture of collection housing. The double measure process usually reveals a number of discrepancies which the library space planner will have

FIGURE 2

A marked layout for a small library. Step one in the measuring process is explained, teams are to begin at opposite ends of the collection. Each team will work on different numbered ranges for step two.

LAYOUT MARKED FOR MEASURING

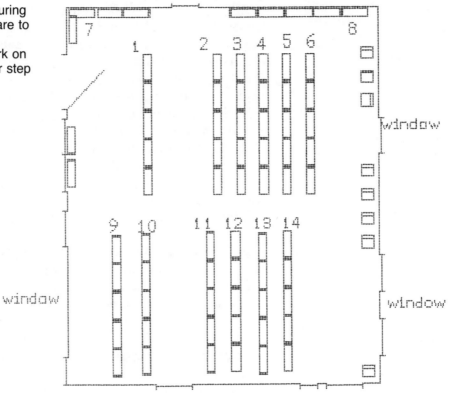

Figure 2. Numbering ranges facilitates dividing measuring between teams: Team 1 will count ranges 1-8, Team 2 will count ranges 9-14.

to check. Verification is facilitated by drawings and notes made on the forms. One member of the team marks the section on the floor plan; the shelving itself may also be marked.

Use a feature of the building, such as a door or a window, as the starting point. The progression of the count should be specific, clear, and carefully explained to all participants. Divide the people doing the counting into teams of two. Assign each team a path to follow and a specific portion of shelving ranges of collection in the library to count. The project manager needs to affix numbers to the ranges and cabinets that the teams are counting ensure that the same range or cabinet is not represented twice in the final tallies.

Record the count on forms similar to those in Figure 3 and Figure 4 and add the forms to the space data file. After the project, the original forms can be discarded and summary sheets included in the file.

Hold training sessions for the data gathering teams. If there are several types and manufacturers of shelving in the library, the project manager may wish to review the shelving types before the teams start so that everyone involved will describe the various types using the same terms and will be able to recognize different types. To insure uniformity, the form could be modified by adding a list of manufacturers' names, or colors or types of shelves, with boxes to check off.

The notes from the teams should include the different characteristics of shelves and supports in each section. For example, many libraries have oversized books on the bottom shelf or baseplate. Others do not place materials on the top or bottom shelf of sections. Sometimes the top shelf is a canopy or cover unsuited for holding books. Some libraries put materials on five shelves, others on six or seven. Some sections might have been cut short to go around a pillar; others may have been made a little longer. If the shelving is 42″ high and the top is used as a consulting shelf, then the presence of consulting shelves should be noted. Notes should also include information about damaged shelves currently in use.

Although marking shelving is recommended, there is no ideal technique for doing this. Tape is a popular choice. When it is not possible to remove the tape immediately, be careful of the kind of tape used. Masking tape and transparent tape leave traces of adhesive on the shelves if left too long or if the room is very warm. Paper labels are virtually impossible to remove. Chalk, however,

---

FIGURE 3. FORM FOR COLLECTION HOUSING

SHELVING RECORD

Range Number _____   Section Number _____

Shelving manufacturer _____

Color _____ End Panels _____ Height _____

Number of Shelves _____ Depth _____ Length _____

Exceptions _____

Notes _____

Date _____   Team _____

can be rubbed off by brushing against the shelves. Marking pencils and magic markers will leave permanent marks. One workable method is to leave a card tucked into each section as it is counted. This, however, can only be used in a closed stack area or at a time when the building is closed and patrons are not in the stacks. Few libraries can keep patrons and staff from rearranging the cards, whether or not it is intentional.

If custom shelving is built into the walls or into the middle of the regular stacks, it should be shown on the layout. Multi-tiered stacks require notations for each tier. Stored collection-housing materials should also be measured and counted. However, if they are being stored because of damage or missing parts, they need not be measured unless repair or restoration is part of the space realignment.

As a result of the marking and measuring activity, a complete and accurate stack layout will be created. The layout should be drawn so section height, color, and manufacturer are visible at a glance. This drawing will help the library space planner visualize alternatives.

CABINETS AND FURNITURE

Collection housing for nonbook formats is often overlooked in the space planning process. Using a form for each item, measure special cases used for maps, photographs, blueprints, microforms, compact discs, microcomputer discs, film, videotapes, phonodiscs, newspapers, and other nonbook materials. Each case should be measured separately, no matter what its original function. For example, the fiche collection may have expanded to such a degree that parts of it are housed in shoe boxes. The shoe box, as soon as it is used to house fiche, is considered part of the library's collection housing equipment and, as such, must be counted and noted.

FIGURE 4. COLLECTION HOUSING: NONSHELVING

Description _____ Location _____

Cabinet number _____

Height _____ Depth _____ Width _____

Drawers/shelves—Number _____ Dimensions _____

Notes _____

Date _____ Team _____

File cabinets are used for vertical file materials and for other sub-collections, such as reserve. They are also used for housing nonprint materials. Individual characteristics of the cabinets should be indicated on a form. It is important to note, for example, if one of the drawers is bent so that it can be repaired or so fewer items go into it. Note the number of drawers per cabinet, their depth, length, width, and whether they contain dividers. It is particularly important to note for the space data file if the cabinet locks, if the key is available, and if it works in the lock.

Nonprint cabinets, like special shelving, are often used for a purpose other than that for which they were designed. It is particularly important, therefore, that the teams carefully note the characteristics of the collection housing in the nonprint area. A letter-size file cabinet used as a microfilm cabinet with cardboard inserted to make dividers must be noted as such. Legal size library cabinets with a rod running through the base of the drawer are common for vertical file materials; since the rods affect the librarian's decision about what can be housed in the cabinets, they are considered a special feature.

The evaluation and measuring teams should be instructed to pay special attention to the physical condition of the individual containers which hold the nonprint materials in order to uncover damages. Damaged cabinets damage library material and vice-versa. For instance, if microfilm is on diazo film rather than silver, a gas is released from the chemicals that can rust the inside of film cabinets and damage the boxes holding the film. The assessment process is designed to discover this condition so that action can be taken during the space implementation.

MEASURING THE COLLECTION

Once you have information about the collection housing, the next step is to gather information about the collection itself. The collection measure must take place before seriously considering any alternatives for collection arrangement or housing. Although consultants can measure and estimate collection sizes, their time is too costly for this. Therefore, the library staff usually assumes full responsibility for the task.

There are various techniques for establishing the actual volume measures. A combination of these techniques provides the most complete picture of actual collection size. Measuring the shelf list, using volume or piece counts from the library's automated systems, information from staff, and linear shelf measures of the collection are all good methods. All of this information is added to the space data file.

Physical Measurements

Collection measures accomplish several functions. They:

> provide information for justifying a project
> assist in locating the collection on floor plans before, during, after the move
> determine what will fit where.

The accuracy of the collection measure determines the success or failure of the reorganization.

The best information on collection size is gained by actually measuring the materials on the shelves in conjunction with circulation data. Or, measure the empty shelf space in each sub-unit and subtract that from the total space to obtain the linear footage of materials to be moved.[2] Carry out this procedure while measuring the collection housing or as a separate step. When collection space is at a premium, the collection measures must be taken inch by inch. In a circulating collection, data must be gathered in a relatively short time frame, preferably one week or less, so the accuracy of the "snapshot" is assured.

Teams using yardsticks or tape measures measure the material wherever it is housed: on shelves, in file cabinets, on tables or stacked on the floor. A form such as that illustrated in Figures 5 and 6 can be used to record the information. Record measurements rounded up to the nearest inch; do not record fractions of inches. One single-faced section of shelving, or range in a larger collection, or one cabinet should be represented on each form. The forms must contain a notation of the call number and the range number where the team is measuring. Color coding the forms is a useful way to delineate collection subdivisions such as reference or law books, special collections, or separate areas. Since this is another project requiring accuracy, especially if shelf space is tight, the double measure is helpful. Once again, the project manager can assign prenumbered forms to the measuring teams to make sure all sections are completed and to avoid significant variations in the results.

Photocopy the forms for measuring the collection housing and for collections back-to-back (Figures 3 with 4, and 5 with 6), so teams only have to go through the collection once. The separate measures of the collection housing and the collection can be worked out so that the teams finish one measure and go right into the other.

Measure subcollections separately, since they require special or separate housing and are usually located apart from the main collections. Examples of subcollections are picture books, uncataloged public access collections, office collections, nonprint materials, academic reserve collections, indexes and abstracts, videotapes, paperbacks, the periodicals display, recorded sound collections, vertical files, rare books, and special collections.

PICTURE BOOKS

Picture books have a high volume count per foot of shelf space and, due to their height and depth, require more space between the shelves on a section than the regular circulating collection. They have heavy in-house usage in addition to a high circulation. Consider a half-full shelf of picture books as a shelf at capacity.

UNCATALOGED PUBLIC-ACCESS COLLECTION

If the uncataloged collection is to remain a part of the library collection in the revised configuration, then it must be measured. This type of material may or may not circulate and information about the status of the collection will not be available from the shelflist counts. Uncataloged materials are usually crowded on the

---

FIGURE 5. FORM FOR COLLECTION MEASURE: BOOKSTOCK

COLLECTION MEASURE: BOOKSTOCK   Location _____

Range Number _____   Section Number _____

Collection measure in inches _____

Start call no. _____   End call no. _____

Number of shelves _____

Notes (special racks, etc.) _____

_____   Team _____

Date _____

shelves, often in no order apparent to a user. Make notes on the collection measure form to indicate method of arrangement, the general condition of the materials, and an indication of what the collection contains.

Examples of uncataloged collections are: a backlog of low-priority materials for which cataloging copy is not yet available; gifts arranged as "help yourself" for patrons; or the paperback collection. It does not matter why the collection is not cataloged. If it is to be retained—therefore requiring a space allocation—then it has to be counted.

OFFICE COLLECTION

Staff offices house a lot of library material. Some of these items are working tools required for the job; others are personal favorites or special collections. The note section on the form should indicate the type of material in the office and whether or not it is cataloged. The occupant of the office can tell the team if the material in the office will have to remain there or if it would be returned to the

---

FIGURE 6. FORM FOR COLLECTION MEASURE: NONBOOK MATERIALS

COLLECTION MEASURE: NONBOOK MATERIALS

Location _____

Type of cabinet/rack/shelf _____

_____ microfilm	_____ Videotapes
_____ microfiche	_____ 16mm film
_____ microcard	_____ 8mm film
_____ vertical files	_____ Records
_____ Videodisc	_____ Diskette
_____ Cassettes	_____ Other
_____ Compact Discs	

Call number/Collection range _____

Number Drawers/shelves _____

Notes _____

Team _____

Date _____

collection if space were available or if the individual's office were moved.

NONPRINT MATERIALS

Accurate information on type of format for nonprint material is important because the cabinets and collection housing for one format may not be suitable for another format. Compact disks, 8 mm films, microcards, videotapes, and microcomputer disks all require different storage cabinets.

When measuring nonprint material, follow the same technique used in measuring the bookstock and use a form similar to that shown in Figure 6. Notes on the contents as well as on the order of the cabinets and housing units are important. The arrangement of the materials in the drawers of the cabinets is also noted on the form. As in the case of the bookstock, define the capacity of the cabinets and how full they are. If some cabinets are nearly empty, it may be possible to combine materials and eliminate one cabinet, especially for formats where zero growth is anticipated.

ACADEMIC RESERVE COLLECTION

The reserve collection in academic librairies is parallel to the bestsellers in the public library: materials in both collections are in high demand. These collections, of course, vary in style and content depending on the institution. Their housing can range from multiple shelves for books to a preponderance of cabinets for copies of articles or reprints or storage for videotapes and disks.

Measure carefully. In many institutions, the reserve materials include such items as floppy disks and videotapes, plus boxes of rocks, maps, globes, models, and other items categorized as realia. In addition, there are the ever-present reprints, papers, photocopied articles, and computer printouts. When there is a choice of when to measure, select the fall reserve collection since it is invariably larger than the spring collection.

INDEXES AND ABSTRACTS

Indexes and abstracts may take up only one shelf or could be spread over many tables and shelves. The notes on the form for these items will be lengthy, since many libraries house prior years of a title in a separate location. Special index tables must be noted and their capacity included. A space decision may have to be made about the number of years of each title housed on each of the index tables, with the earlier volumes going into storage or onto adjacent shelves.

If there are no index tables, a note can refer to any special shelving arrangements for the frequently consulted index materials. More and more indexing information is now handled on CD-ROM or database searching. If the latter is the case, the microcomputer will be included in the collection-housing portion of the measuring process. CD-ROM stations are also considered part of the equipment, and a special notation should indicate that this equipment must be located near the reference desk or other public service area.

PERIODICAL AND NEWSPAPER DISPLAY

The periodical display requires attention as a subcollection. Sometimes all of the current titles are displayed on hinged periodical shelving, with the back issues stored under the current one; other arrangements are to have current periodicals on special display shelving, with the back issues stored elsewhere; another arrangement may be only a few titles on a special display piece of furniture. Because of the difference in the number and manner of display of periodical titles, the note section will be especially important. Newspapers are frequently included in the current periodicals area. If special furniture is used, this should be noted in the collection housing. If the papers are housed on regular shelving, then be sure to include the space used in the collection measure.

RECORDED SOUND COLLECTION

When measuring and counting phonodisk or CD housing, note how full they are and whether it is possible to browse among the disks. Even if the collection is not in a public access area, space will have to be delineated for it in the new configuration, so it must be measured. Also measure and count cassette holdings and "kits" of materials. Circulation records should be checked since some recordings will be signed out. If the shelflist measure is to be used, an inventory is essential since recordings usually have a high loss rate.

VERTICAL FILES

Count the number of cabinets and drawers and measure the space the files consume in the cabinets. Indicate on the forms if the files are kept in special file folders or regular file folders, and if the files are legal or letter size. The note should also include information about which files are overloaded or are in need of splitting and reconfiguration.

RARE BOOKS AND SPECIAL COLLECTIONS

There is no universal library definition of "special collections." The definition in one library may be "rare or archival quality materials" and in another "material in need of special treatment because it is likely to be stolen." Some special collections are housed together and separated from other library materials because of the conditions attached to a gift. Reading rooms with small collections devoted to a specific theme may contain a special collection; materials are cataloged separately and therefore form a nuclear collection of subject materials. Some school libraries have special collections which are the result of a one-time purchase by special funds. Special funds awarded to a library may have a contingency attached requiring a separate location for these materials.

There are always some special collections housed near the reference desk. In some libraries this collection changes content as the year progresses; in others, it consists of the ready-reference materials; in still others, it is kept in a locked cabinet for security. Note the locked container when the collection housing information is gathered; the contents of the container are part of the library collection and their measurement takes place during the collection measure.

For the purposes of space planning, *any section of the collection housed in a location other than its regular call number sequence must be counted separately*. If one of the goals of the project is to incorporate this collection back into the regular sequence, it is necessary to measure it at this stage of the project. This includes, in addition to the collections we have identified, special sections of oversized or undersized materials, or special series which may be pulled out and shelved separately. The collections in areas of the library containing special arrangements of new books or books on display are counted as a special collection.

Rare books kept in a separate location with temperature control and special security will have to be moved or shifted item by item using special procedures. Therefore, in the collection assessment, they should be counted and measured individually. Conduct a title-by-title inventory prior to the move and annotate the shelflist. Use this information to maintain the security of the collection as the volumes are moved.

Measuring the Shelflist

One technique for measuring the size of a library collection is to measure the shelflist. The standard "one inch of shelflist cards for 100 volumes" is useful where the time required for a shelf measurement is not possible. This technique is most accurate in a large collection with a correspondingly large shelflist. Statistical samples may be taken of call-number ranges to verify accuracy of shelflist measures. An estimate of the space needed for each call-number range is required to avoid shifting the collection frequently after the planned move. There are, however, some factors which will affect the totals.

Without a recent inventory, the accuracy of a shelflist count is questionable because there is no information on the percentage of cards in the shelflist that do not represent volumes on the shelves. Records of resolution of the inventory problems are also useful because the records show the estimated percentage of books missing from the shelves. Many libraries use a statistical sampling methodology to define the estimated percentage of missing materials. These sample techniques can be accurate, but problems occur when a sample is not representative, or there are errors in the calculations, or the method of selecting the sample was inaccurate.

The best sampling technique is called systematic sampling wherein every X (10th, 20th or 100th) card in the shelflist is tested to determine if the item the card represents is missing from the collection. The sample selected in this manner will retain the characteristics of the distribution of the collection over the call-number ranges.

The number of cards to be sampled can be determined by using the formula $N = (zA/e)^2 p(1-p)$. In this formula, N is the number of items to be tested; p is the estimated percentage of items missing from the collection provided by the library space planner. Since .03 or 3 percent missing is considered a large amount for library collections, this is a good figure to use if the library space planner has no idea of the number of items missing. $(ZA/e)^2$ is the degree of statistical confidence in the estimate. If the space planner wants a 99 percent probability that the sample will be different from the actual losses by no more than five percent, use $e = .05$ and $ZA = 2.58$. Common probabilities are 95 percent ($ZA = 1.96$) and 90 percent ($ZA = 1.64$). The product of this formula will be the total number of items to be sampled. For example, if $N = 100$ and there are 10,000 cards in the shelflist, then an accurate estimate of the number of items missing from the library can be obtained by sampling every 100 cards.

When this formula is used, the result will be a range or a confidence interval. The proper way to state the results is, "Based on the sample, we can say with (90 percent or 99 percent or 95 percent) confidence that the percentage of items missing will fall between 0.05 and 1.0 percent." The space planner can then make the choice between the lowest and highest percentage on this confidence interval for each call-number range.

The record-keeping practices of the library will define the "shelflist" for data collection purposes. One standard definition of shelflist is a record of all of the library holdings exactly as they are shelved. When this is used, the library keeps records by filing all cards in the same order as the books or materials on the shelves. For example, if the oversized collection is in a separate section, the cards for it are filed in a separate section of the shelflist catalog.

Another interpretation of a shelflist is a record in call number sequence of all the library holdings, regardless of prefix or format. In this case, the shelflist will not yield an accurate record of all of the shelving needs without additional calculations. The reference and nonprint materials records may be interfiled with the circulating materials, as will records for other items in the library collection which are housed in locations separate from the circulating collection. One way to arrive at an estimate using this type of shelflist is to use a combination of measuring techniques.

First, measure the shelflist using a ruler and "one inch equals 100 volumes" rule of thumb and collect the measures by call number range. Next, measure the collections which are housed in separate locations. Subtract this figure from the first. If the library interfiles print and nonprint, check the number of entries for nonprint materials and subtract this from the total. Since the shelflist measure technique involves determining volume counts, check the number of volumes in the nonprint format and use this as the figure to subtract.

Each of these separate section measures must be in call-number sequence. For example, the total number of volumes in the reference collection cannot be subtracted from the total number in the library collection to arrive at the number to allocate space for the circulating collection because both collections are arranged in call-number sequence and the adjustment might be off. Separate the call-number ranges into subsets; the smaller the shelflist call-number range breakdown, the more accurate the information.

Other Measures

Most online circulation or cataloging systems provide title and volume counts of holdings in the system. If records for the collection are all online, knowing the file maintenance procedures is important. If it is possible to get only part of the data from online records, then a combination of measuring options will have to be used.

Circulation systems often record the volume counts, as opposed to the title counts. The totals from the system may have to be adjusted if the system does not include noncirculating material or if noncirculating materials are included but the records do not yield enough information to provide accurate volume counts.

The method of registering periodical volumes in the system is most often open to count discrepancies. Trying to extrapolate from a holdings record without additional information is a poor space planning practice. Sometimes, the records do not reflect the format of the title. Holdings of *The New York Times* on microfilm requires different housing than paper copy holdings of *Life Magazine*. Online holdings statements also may not distinguish between formats. If the mixed formats are shelved together the situation becomes further complicated.

Serials present a similar problem for library space assessment. Titles are often entered under the name of the series, and the record may or may not include the number of volumes or pieces for the single bibliographic record. The same problem applies to encyclopedias and law materials; unless they are recorded as individual volumes in a circulation system, the only way to get a good measure of the number of volumes is to count the entries on the shelflist card or to measure the volumes on the shelves.

Since most online systems have been created for priorities other than space planning, disparities in system volume counts and physical volume counts are predictable. The space planner needs to identify the discrepancy and adjust measuring techniques to reflect the characteristics of the system in use in the library being measured.

WORKING FROM CIRCULATION RECORDS

The circulation record is first used in conjunction with inventory findings. The inventory, ultimately, provides the planner with an estimate of the number of volumes off the shelves and not accounted for in the circulation records. If the item is circulating, then the item is not missing. The planner can assume it will return, and shelf space must be allocated for it.

Circulation records also show the number of volumes in a suspended status—for instance, long overdue items, snags, or missing books—and so provide information about books or materials not available but requested by patrons. The library definition of suspended status will determine if the items can be assumed to be part of the collection or if they should be considered lost and thus not considered in space allocations. These figures are similar in purpose to the percentage missing defined by the inventory. In order to have the most meaning for shelf-space allocation, the figures should be divided in call number order.

If the data are not available in call-number order but are in a lump sum, then estimate the call-number range distribution from the lump sum by extrapolating percentages from circulation information. If 50 percent of the materials in circulation are from one call-number range, then there is a good chance that 50 percent of the missing and overdue items will also be from that call-number sequence. If this information is not available on a regular basis, gather it during a sample period so it can be used for projections. The American National Standards Institute's Z39.7 standard makes use of a "typical week," defined as a five- to seven-day period in the operating year of a library which most closely represents the average activity. A "typical week" can be selected for a sample size and projections based on figures from this time period.

USING SHELF CAPACITY STANDARDS

It is possible to estimate the number of volumes per single-faced section of the collection using standard measurements if there is not enough staff and time to do an up-to-the-inch shelf measure. The subject arrangements based on the Library of Congress, Dewey, or National Library of Medicine classification schedules are the most frequently used. Libraries which have devised or modified classification schemes for special subjects should define their own standards of volumes per single-faced section. Within a standard classification system, the numbers of volumes per single-faced section vary from 125[3] to 140 for an "average library."[4] An error in estimation creates problems which will surface in the new shelving configuration. For instance, when a call-number class splits into two or three locations, there is a corresponding loss of subject access.

Library shelves are considered full when three-quarters of the shelf is occupied; they have reached what is known as "working capacity." One-quarter shelf remains which can be used for some small-scale shifting required by the normal process of circulation and collection growth. Any shelf loaded beyond the three quarter mark is too full. However, back runs of periodicals and caselaw which will not grow can filled to the ends.

To determine a local library standard, count the volumes actually on the shelves in 20 randomly selected single-faced sections. Use 50 sections in a larger library. Random selection, necessary to obtain statistical significance, is accomplished by selecting sections in no specific sequence. Put the books in order and straighten the section before counting, but do not add or subtract volumes. Divide the total number of volumes by the number of sections sampled to arrive at the arithmetic mean. This number becomes the local library standard.

INFORMATION FROM THE STAFF

Information from staff members is valuable during the process of measuring the collection; it is information not available elsewhere. The library staff member who works in circulation or stack maintenance and serves patrons all day, every day, can provide information about the materials off of the shelves. A good circulation clerk knows the call-number ranges where patrons are requesting material which cannot be located. This information will support the statistical measures undertaken as part of the space assessment process.

PROJECTING FUTURE GROWTH

When planning to move bookstock and other materials, the determination of the space required for future collection growth will enable the new space configuration to work. One way to define this growth is to identify the net number of items added to the collection during the past year and plan to add at least that number each year. Enter this figure in the space data file as a projection. A more reliable technique is to average the number of pieces added during the past five years and consider this the annual growth figure in the space data file.

In a crowded library, every attempt should be made to tie the anticipated growth to a specific call-number sequence. For example, if the projection is to add 100,000 items each year, it will help to know that 90 percent of these items are book materials and five percent are videotapes or microforms. The percentages can be broken down further—55 percent of the book materials may be fiction, ten percent science, and so on.

Predicting the growth of the periodicals collection is difficult. Staff at the University of South Carolina Medical Library measured the last complete available year of all currently received titles to determine the yearly growth rate, in inches, for each title. Excluded from the process were titles not bound, not shelved in the periodicals collection, and not currently received.[5]

The *Bowker Annual* provides information on publishing output in the U.S. and can be used to define growth. Using the number of new volumes added in a specific subject area as the numerator, divide by the number published in that subject area during the reporting period. Multiply the result by 100 to get the percentage of publishing output the library adds during a year. Again, a more realistic figure for local purposes may be obtained by averaging over a five-year period.

Financial information should be used for growth planning. If the book budget has increased or decreased from year to year, define a relationship between budget change and change in total volumes. For example, assume a budget has increased by ten percent, but the number of volumes added has decreased by five percent. Unless the budget increases 15 percent in the next year, the number of volumes added will again decrease from the current year.

Preparing Alternate Layouts

Accurate and comprehensive data are the basis for decisions made on the reallocation of collection growth space and also define the possible space utilization alternatives. Not only do the data point out what collections will fit where in the initial planning stages; they are also useful for the detailed layouts required to accomplish a successful move.

Spreadsheet packages are effectively used to tabulate the collected data, view several layout options, and plan for more growth space in the parts of the collection growing more quickly. *Electronic Spreadsheets for Libraries* presents three spreadsheets that take into account the number of items per shelf, the number of shelves per section, the floor area occupied by each section and the aisle widths. Cell formulas are included.[6]

REFERENCES

1. Ralph M. Daehn, "The Measurement and Projection of Shelf Space" *Collection Management,* 4 (Winter 1982): 28-9.
2. Judith Compton Ellis, "Planning and Executing a Major Bookshift/Move Using an Electronic Spreadsheet" *College & Research Libraries News,* 5 (May 1988): 283.
3. Philip D. Leighton and David C. Weber, *Planning Academic and Research Library Buildings,* 2nd Ed. (Chicago: American Library Association, 1986): 559.
4. John Boll, "To Grow or Not to Grow" *LJ Special Report #15* (New York: R. R. Bowker, 1980): 16.
5. Barbara A. Carlson, "Using Lotus 1-2-3 to Shift and Maintain a Serials Collection" *The Serials Librarian,* 13 (December 1987): 43.
6. Lawrence W. S. Auld, *Electronic Spreadsheets for Libraries* (Phoenix, Ariz.: Oryx Press, 1986): 77-100.

3 THE SPACE CRUNCH: ALTERNATIVES

When new space is not forthcoming, the space planner must examine alternatives to existing collection housing practices. A number of traditional options are available: installation of compact shelving; conversion of periodicals and other print materials to microformat; establishment of a off-site storage facility; adoption of the zero-growth concept or institution of a weeding program; and implementation of nontraditional shelving methods.

Other options have emerged that are gaining favor: stronger resource sharing programs, use of CD-ROM and using technology to replace in-house collections. Some of these options involve the library's collection housing; others involve the library's collection development and retention policies; and others change the way the acquisitions budget is expended. None of the options are inexpensive, but with new construction costs averaging over $70 per square foot and with library collections continuing to grow and new services increasing, alternative approaches to housing collections are often the only choices for finding space.

The following discussion of alternatives pinpoints areas that require extra attention when gathering space data and identifies advantages and disadvantages of each option. As the reader will see, alternatives for the collection rarely involve the collection alone. Other aspects of the library building and operations must be considered.

COMPACT SHELVING

"Movable compact shelving provides a successful, permanent answer to the storage and preservation problems afflicting many libraries. Their advantages greatly outweigh their minor disadvantages. Any library which installs such a system will find that it has made a prudent and cost-effective investment."[1]

"Formerly installed in closed-access collections, compact shelving is more and more frequently installed for public access collections."[2] Compact shelving maximizes collection storage space, usually doubling storage capacity. The sixth stack addition at the University of Illinois, containing compact shelving, has a storage capacity of 28.4 volumes per square foot of floor area, as compared to 12.1 volumes in the other stack facilities.[3]

Compact shelving eliminates the aisles between each range of shelving and a number of ranges use one "moving" aisle. The ranges move on tracks, singly or several ranges at once. Installations are either electrical or mechanical assist; the costs for electrical are substantially higher than those for mechanical.

If installation of compact shelving is under consideration, the load-bearing weight of the floor has to be carefully evaluated.[4] Before proceeding with this option, ensure that the floor can handle at least 300 pounds per square foot, live load. Structural modifications may be necessary to increase the building's load bearing capacity. Consult a structural engineer before committing to a compact shelving installation. Do not assume that the basement floor can handle the weight. In one building, circa 1928, the engineers insisted on taking core samples of the floor in the prospective compact shelving area to ensure that compact shelving could be safely installed.

Sales representatives of companies that make compact shelving will be able to provide a layout and accurate cost estimates for specific library situations.[5] Electrical compact shelving has special installation requirements for electrical wiring and power sources.

Two major considerations in layout planning are the lighting sources and the traffic patterns. The aisles should open in a place where lighting is adequate to read materials when taken off the shelves. An area may be unsuited to compact shelving unless the lighting is redesigned. Traffic patterns must be planned to allow both people and book trucks into the aisles. If a high-access collection, such as current periodical holdings, is placed in compact shelving, the traffic load will be higher, requiring more movable aisles than if low-use, older holdings are placed in the compact shelving or if they are used for closed access storage.

Part of the planning process for compact shelving installation should be a well-structured study of usage for portions of the collection targeted for the compact shelving. Since the number of aisles required to provided access to the collection affects the amount of shelving placed in the available space and, therefore, storage capacity, it is critical to plan adequate access while still maximizing storage space.

Compact shelving has its disadvantages:

- The floor may not be able to handle the load, and, if structural reinforcement is required, the initial investment can be significant.
- In a full-to-capacity facility, there are enormous difficulties

in off-loading 60,000 to 100,000 volumes and storing them in retrievable order while the compact shelving is installed.

- The addition of any electrical or mechanical equipment requires an ongoing repair and maintenance plan, plus the investment costs in the initial installation.
- If a future planner wishes to assign this space to another function, the presence of compact shelving can make this task almost impossible since it requires virtually permanent floor track installations.
- Patrons may present stiff resistance to the shelving because browsing is affected. Detractors of compact shelving believe it alters the atmosphere and design of the library to such an extent that the ability of the library to fulfill its mission is affected.

The advantages of compact shelving are numerous:

- The increased bookstock capacity in one location is the greatest advantage. Collection housing capacity is nearly doubled in the same amount of space. The life of each book is extended because less dust gets into the bookstock and the lights are not always shining on each volume.
- Collection security can be enhanced by the controlled access inherent in a compact-shelving installation. Security for patrons and staff is also improved as there are fewer aisles and cul-de-sacs to patrol.
- Compact shelving is often most effective when used to house less-frequently-required materials. An active section of the collection may require too many aisles to make the installation cost-beneficial.

CONVERTING TO MICROFORMAT

Conversion to microformat is an especially attractive solution in a library with large holdings of older bound periodicals and in law collections with extensive retrospective case law. Since this is one of the most logical and available alternatives for periodical and case law storage, it has been discussed at length in the library literature. Although many investigations of microform conversion consider only the periodical format because of the extensive commercial availability of periodical back runs, some consideration should be given to converting other areas of the collection. Special subject collections are also available in microformat.[6]

The cost factor is significant in microform conversion. When the university-wide Library Planning Office of the University of California investigated space options, three microform options were assessed: microform conversion of all materials not used in the past ten years, estimated at a cost of $35 per volume; replacement of bound periodical volumes with film or fiche if the titles were available commercially, an option which was more costly than central storage; and subscribing to current journals in microform as well as as print, but retaining microform copy rather than binding. The third option was the only one providing cost savings for the university situation.[7]

In *Microforms: the Librarians View, 1978-1979*, Alice Bahr points out the cost savings available if a library acquires journals from publishers who have special plans to make microforms available at lower costs. The Pergamon plan, for example, offers current issues at 80 percent of the hard-copy price and year-end editions at 50 percent.[8]

The question of the commercial availability of periodical titles is important. Some publishers require up to two years to elapse before the title is available for purchase in microformat; others will sell the microform copy to a library only if a current subscription is maintained. Many monographs and some periodicals are never commercially available in microformat, and the library must arrange filming if it selects this option.

The option of filming materials other than periodicals should be part of any microform conversion investigation. Some special collections are good candidates for microform conversion. Investigate contracts with commercial companies to film segments of the special collections or those "special" files on topics that seems to grow of their own volition. Since medical records, bank records, and countless other files are microfilmed, use of film and paper copies from film is no longer a problem for many patrons.

When contracting for microfilming, carefully consider the information on the header as well as the indexing and arrangement. Use an in-house data base management program such as RBase or DBase to produce an online index or print index specifying storage cabinet drawer numbers or utilize the online catalog as the collection access tool.

Initial costs for microform conversion are high. Staff time is required to select the titles to be converted and should be calculated and added to the initial conversion cost estimates. Other costs are incurred in weeding the bound volume collections, changing records, and disposing of the materials. A high initial investment is often required to pay for new reader and printer equipment and storage cabinets, and the initial order of microforms. If the filming is going to be done "in-house," costs for cameras, staff, film, and processing must be taken into account.

In addition, the project will have to be large enough to enable recovery of the space required for processing. Ongoing costs are in equipment maintenance and replacement; decent reading and printing equipment is a must. The acceptance of the format by patrons and staff is contingent on good equipment, proper lighting, and easily followed directions for using equipment and finding materials.

Collection-space savings are tremendous as a result of microform conversion, even though the reader equipment will occupy space. Electrical requirements will increase for the library building if this option is selected. Microform readers do not draw much electricity, but inadequate electricity leads to blurred images and effectively limits the use of material. Storage space is needed for extra bulbs and reader-printer supplies. Coin-operated copying earns revenue but requires coin change, security for the cash box, and maintenance of the coin mechanism. Because a cabinet full of microforms is heavy, the load-bearing weight of the floors must be sufficient. This weight factor is sometimes ignored in the rush to evaluate floor loading for books. Ask the structural engineer to review the microform storage area when evaluating other aspects of the facility.

Effective publicity for a microform conversion project is very important. Staff and patrons alike may object when the library discards the bound holdings. The implementation process may have to be phased in over a period of time. One compromise is to stop binding journals after a certain date and, from that date forward, purchase microform. Another option is purchase of microform for bound holdings ten years old and older. In this way savings are realized, and a gradual retrospective conversion is implemented. Some librarians have chosen the occasion of a move to a new building to make the change and discard bound items. If an addition is being constructed or the interior space is being renovated specifically for microforms, the change can be implemented at one time and patron and staff adjustment to microforms will be part of the overall adjustment to the new facility.

Microform conversion can recover significant floor space. However, a massive conversion project invariably involves a major collection shift as the type of space required for cabinets and readers is different from that needed to house books.

Users' acceptance is greatly dependent on the environment created to accommodate their needs. A patron using a microform reader needs room to take notes, good copying equipment, and lighting sufficient for taking notes and yet not contributing to glare on the screen. Prior to selecting this option, consult additional sources so that all aspects of a microform conversion are thought through.[9]

OFFSITE STORAGE

In some cases, storing part of the library's holdings may be the best way to provide collection growth space. When the library's collection development policy specifies in-depth collections in a subject area, as is often the case in academic institutions, or when the available space is so small that only a service point and workspace is available, as is the case in some special libraries, storage should be investigated. Establishment of a storage facility at Adelphi University was chosen over weeding, microform conversion, or increased reliance on interlibrary loan.[10] California State University opted for storage using industrial storage technology.[11] "Storage facilities, once an interim solution for colleges and universities [that] couldn't currently afford new library buildings, have now become the common answer to the need for increased shelf space in academic libraries. The idea of providing low-cost storage space for lesser-used materials has struck an economic chord in the higher education community as money for library additions or new buildings dwindles."[12]

Collection storage signifies closed or limited access, scheduled or limited retrieval, and use of a shelving method that maximizes the collection storage space. Storing part of the holdings creates growth space for the collections not stored and/or frees up space for service expansion. Entire call-number ranges or subcollections can be placed in one location, where temperature control may be better and collection security is increased.

A major decision is determining which materials to store if storage space is available for only part of the collection. Staff members at the University of California elected to place all low-use materials in a remote storage facility. "Low use" was defined as an item that had not circulated in the past ten years.[13] Other librarians have divided the collection by subject and stored entire subject areas, thus reducing the costs of record-changing. A local usage study will provide an estimate of retrieval projected activity. Selection of materials for storage can be based on:

- publication date
- the type of materials, such as maps or newspapers
- the last date of circulation
- the subject area

A perfect method for selecting materials to be stored does not exist. No matter what is stored, there almost always will be demand for it. The decision was made at one academic library to store bound periodicals ten years old and older under the assumption that the materials were little used. The equivalent of one FTE clerical required to retrieve the materials was a surprise and had a significant staffing impact. Retrieving items costs money in vehicles, containers, staff time, altering records, and record-keeping. A micro program may alleviate record-keeping paperwork, but the other functions remain constant.

The added cost of time to the user and the staff for retrieving materials in storage is partially offset by the greater accessibility to that part of the collection not in storage and an enhanced ability to keep this collection in order. Storing fragile materials under controlled conditions increases their life span. The general condition of the stacks will improve when a portion of the total collection has been removed. The open-access collection will be easier to use because of decreased crowding on the shelves.

One of the greatest disadvantages of storage is the loss of immediate book availability. Because users may object to the loss of browsing capabilities, an additional program to increase availability of sections of the collection might be needed. Compromise is possible if a clamor arises. Library staff can bring a selection of materials to a special reading area and leave it there for a few weeks. With adequate publicity, this compromise has a high probability of success. Special stack passes allowing browsing in the storage area is another option. The pass system necessitates a library attendant during scheduled hours. This is not considered open access since the collection is not available all hours and the number of users is restricted. If special stack passes will be part of the operation, the storage area or facility should be designed with staff work space, and the arrangement of the collection becomes more important.

Costs of start-up and of moving items to storage must be considered in addition to ongoing maintenance and staffing costs. And more money must be spent to make the facility usable and pay for shelving, furnishings, paint, window repair, and new lock systems keyed to the library master. A book security system may have to be installed, as well as intrusion security system.

An additional copy machine may be necessary if a large amount of material is sent to the offsite storage facility, especially if it is far away or if the library is unable to provide courier service. Investigate telefacsimile transmission as an element of offsite storage. Telephone lines will have to be installed if staff are expected to be at the facility for any length of time; intercom capabilities are a minimal requirement. Staff hours will have to be assigned for shelving and maintenance. If software is developed, electricity and a microcomputer must be part of the offsite equipment. There must also be access to the circulation system and online catalog.

A microcomputer program using one of the commercially available data base management program can be created as part of the planning. This program, coupled with the library circulation system, will enable meaningful management reports to be produced. Canned spreadsheet-based inventory control programs are also applicable for library offsite storage management. The objective of the software is to record the costs and activities associated with accessing the stored segment of the collection.

Storage is frequently the favored option when collection space is scarce; occasionally, selection of this option is imposed by external factors. One common scenario involves the "gift" of space to the library in response to the library-crowding problems. "Gift" space is sometimes selected to go to the library because it is unsuited for the needs of the organization or community. Since it is often remote to the library, storage of part of the collection in this gift space may be its ideal use.

SHELVING OPTIONS

Nontraditional methods of shelving bookstock may be introduced to increase collection growth space and ease crowding. Several of these options are summarized below. For more details about each alternative in an academic setting, consult the *LJ Special Report*, "To Grow or Not to Grow."[14] The factors identified by Boll are applicable to all types of libraries.

Many of these options are utilized in collection storage areas to maximize storage space. Some options are also feasible for open-access collections.

SHELVING BY SIZE

Library collections with undersized and oversized volumes shelved in separate sections have taken one step in the direction of shelving by size. When the size breakdown is used for all of the bookstock, the first section may contain nine shelves and the smallest volumes, while the final sections contain three or four shelves. The remainder of the collection is in order by size, in between the two. This option maximizes the use of existing collection housing and floor space.

Shelving by size is also a good way to crowd materials into a collection storage facility. Studies conducted by academic libraries considering size-shelving for remote storage use four or more size groups. When collections are shelved in size groups, between three percent and 25 percent is added to the overall shelf space capacity, depending on the height of the shelves.[15]

The disadvantages of this method are:

- loss of subject access provided by one call-number sequence and the need to provide extensive stack guides
- the time and effort involved in identifying correct order, shifting the collection, and assigning the correct size category to each item on the shelves
- loss of browsing capability.

Costs involve the one-time investment for total reshifting: the relabeling of cards, books, and records; producing signs and flyers and retraining staff and patrons. New shelves will have to be purchased—an additional start-up cost. Plan an extensive, continuing user education campaign if shelving by size is selected.

FORE-EDGE AND FLAT SHELVING

All materials are shelved on the edges of their covers, making the books spines parallel to the shelves rather than the usual perpendicular arrangement. Using this method, at least two shelves can be added to a standard 90″ high section, increasing available space by approximately 28 percent. To preserve the books, the spines must be placed on the shelf, obscuring the call numbers. If spines are "face up," books are damaged because of the stress of the text block pulling away from the casing. Browsing is difficult since call numbers are not visible. Shelving on the fore-edge does maintain call-number sequence, and the initial move or shift of the collection is not as extensive as with some other options.

Long runs of legal materials, such as early case law, lend themselves to a version of fore-edge shelving. The volume number is written on the edges of the books in large print. Each shelf is filled using a strict fore-edge arrangement, or books are placed flat on the shelves with the bottom facing outward. Using this method, a shelf normally housing 17-18 law books can hold up to 25 volumes, a 28 percent increase.

Because shelf space is retrieved, it may be desirable to give serious consideration to the fore-edge shelving method. Perhaps fore-edge shelving is best for sections of the collection that do not receive heavy use. Because of the long-term damage to the materials, fore-edge shelving is not recommended for portions of the collection slated for indefinite retention.

MOVING EXISTING SHELVING

Decreasing the aisle widths by moving the ranges closer together is another way to recoup floor space and maximize collection housing. The gain in floor space allows construction of additional ranges. Recovery of space is a function of the size of the library, shelving configuration, and building design. Reducing three-foot aisles to two-foot aisles results in a gain of 20 percent more collection space.

The advantage to revising the aisle configuration is the gain of collection space without compromising the browsing function. The primary disadvantage is in limited accessibility, especially for the mobility-impaired patron. Check state building codes to ensure that the proposed project is in compliance. If the aisles are reduced too much, book trucks may not fit and browsing may be possible in theory only. If this option is chosen, consider adopting a limited-access policy and provide stack paging service.

Costs will be for labor, repair, and replacement parts for disas-

FIGURES 1 AND 2

Design Alternative #3 (Figures 1 and 2) is another variation of the space shown in Chapter 1.

DESIGN ALTERNATIVE #3

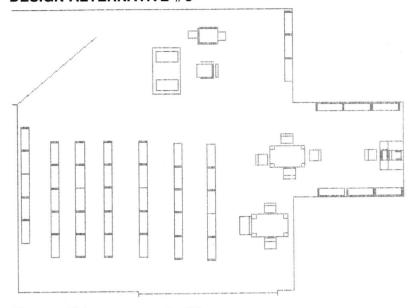

Figure 1. This arrangement will house approximately 10,000 volumes.

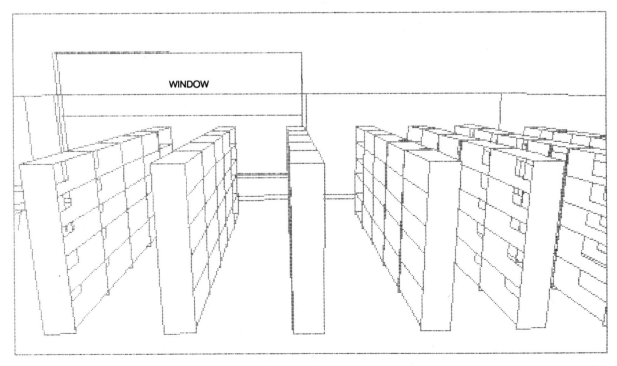

Figure 2. View from the service desk before aisle reduction (Figures 3 and 4 on page 64).

FIGURES 3 AND 4

Increasing capacity by moving the
ranges closer together must be
weighed against the crowded atmosphere in the stacks .

DESIGN ALTERNATIVE #4

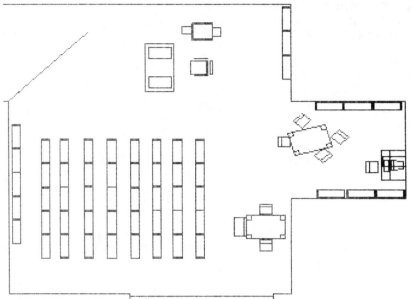

Figure 3. Moving ranges closer together makes
room for approximately 12,500 volumes, but creates
narrow aisles.

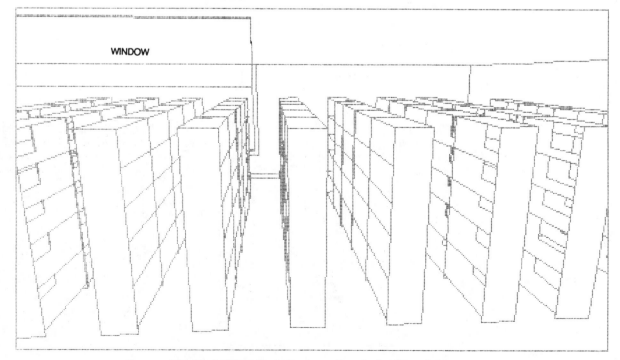

Figure 4. View from the service desk after aisles
have been reduced.

sembled shelving and for the purchase of any new shelving. Extensive collection shifting is involved as ranges are emptied, moved, then refilled. This must be done in a closely coordinated progression of events. Carefully plan the revised stack layout to allow sufficient light in the aisles for browsing and reshelving. There may be an additional cost to attach track lighting to the tops of the ranges or to realign the lighting fixtures. When the tentative layout is created, the light fixtures are drawn in to identify potential problems.

The elimination of cross aisles between ranges is another possibility for increasing collection space while retaining the browsing functions of the library. Less space will be recovered using this technique than if the ranges are moved closer together, but it recovers space for a few years' growth. The disadvantage is the extra-long ranges of bookshelves, which decreases mobility within the library. Costs involve the labor for shifting and additional shelving. The floor treatment investigation, outlined in Chapter 4, must be completed before this option is seriously considered. If carpet or floor treatment has been installed around ranges, it may not be possible to move them without replacing the carpet. This will increase costs considerably and may effectively eliminate the option.

DOUBLE-SHELVING BOOKS

Two rows of books may be housed on one shelf if the shelf is at least 10″ wide; shelves 8″ wide are too narrow for double-shelving. Of course, since some areas of the collection have bigger volumes, this method cannot be used in every section. Subject areas most easily double-shelved are fiction, literature, and history.

The disadvantages of double-shelving in an open-access collection are obvious; browsing is reduced, and difficulty in locating materials is increased. Access is facilitated if double shelving is used for series such as legal case law or back runs of bound reports or periodicals. Shelf reading will have to be done more often, and good graphics are a must. On the plus side, space is doubled in some areas of the collection. The material may be more difficult to locate, but at least it will be in the same area.

The costs involved in double-shelving are in acquiring enough shelves of the correct width, shifting the collection to the new configuration, the new signs, and staff training. Ongoing costs are incurred by more frequent and time-consuming shelf reading and added patron training and orientation.

ADDING TO THE UPRIGHTS

Another option for getting the most out of existing space is to extend the shelving uprights. Depending on how much height is added, an additional one to two shelves can be hung off each single-faced section. The feasibility of this option depends on the type of shelving used by the library, plus ceiling height. Some types of shelving cannot be extended. However, once completed, expansion space is built in throughout the stacks, thus eliminating the requirements of a major collection shift. It can then be shifted within sections, gradually.

Factors to consider include:

> cost of the added shelf-unit pieces, including extenders and shelves, the equipment and labor to fasten them, and stools or ladders to reach the higher shelves
> redrilling the shelving cross-ties
> evaluating existing lighting and air circulation in advance, since the costs to alter or upgrade may be prohibitively expensive
> consulting with an engineer about the expense and feasibility of this option.

WAREHOUSE SHELVING

Warehouse shelving can save space in some situations, but should be used only in closed-access collections because books must be stored three to four rows deep on each shelf in order to maximize the shelf space. It should never be used in an open-access library. A unit 30″ x 36″ with seven shelves yields storage space for 63 linear feet of materials (three rows) or 84 feet if four rows deep. One double-faced section of library shelving provides 42 linear shelf-feet.

Although a section of warehouse shelving occupies more floor space than a double-faced section of library shelving, the storage space gain outweighs this disadvantage. It is by far the most efficient way to store manuscripts.

Warehouse shelving is less attractive than standard library shelving and not as flexible. Added, special-purpose shelf features such as display fronts, special frames, and AV supports are not found in warehouse shelving. Costs include:

- the initial investment and the shift
- the cost of bookends, since warehouse shelves do not have end braces
- the cost of retrieving materials from storage

- the initial investment, including the cost of bringing heat, humidity, and lighting to a level at which collection disintegration is not accelerated.

ZERO-GROWTH AND WEEDING

Another space-saving option is the adoption of the zero-growth concept or the institution of an ongoing weeding program. Although lack of collection growth space may be the driving force behind adopting either of these options, the library administration must first review and possibly revise the mission statement since these policies and practices modify the content of the collection and affect service delivery.

Richard Trueswell studied the use of academic library collections and determined that most of the materials in a library are never used.[16] The Pitt Study on library use supported this hypothesis.[17] Lancaster discusses the age of materials as a predictor of use and states: "The librarian's interest in obsolescence is practical rather than theoretical. If use declines with age, one should be able to discard items on the basis of age or at least move older items to less accessible and less costly storage."[18]

Zero-growth is a collection development policy with the theoretical goal of maintaining a constant collection size. If a library is successfully following this option, the collection will always consume the same amount of space. Many libraries in Great Britain have adopted the zero-growth concept because lack of collection-growth space in libraries has been a major issue for some time. However, the concept involves withdrawing an item for each one added. Collections will have to be shifted within the fixed space allocated, as zero-growth rarely means add a volume and then pull one in the same call-number range. The zero-growth concept has not been embraced in the United States, as evidenced by the numerous additions, renovations, and new building projects listed each year in the December issue of *Library Journal*.

Weeding—the process of reviewing the collection title-by-title and deciding to discard items—is another policy option that can be used to assure collection growth space. There are several versions of weeding. A public library may routinely weed and discard any item from the circulating collection that has not been borrowed for two years. An academic library may closely monitor enrollment and curricular development; it may weed materials as a major is eliminated or a curriculum changes direction.

Extensive weeding can be used to retrieve space or to precipitate a collection shift. Weeding, however, rarely retrieves significant amounts of growth space for collections unless a volume goal has been set and the project is on-going and part of the collection management policy.

OPTICAL DISK TECHNOLOGY

"Optical disk storage technology is among the most recent computer technologies to enter the library community. Characterized by extremely high-density data storage, optical disks offer storage capacities measured in millions of characters per square inch. These disks offer the potential for significant savings in shelf space in a library community where the cost of space is always increasing. The computer systems developed to utilize these disks offer improved search access to materials at high rates of speed."[19]

Although the optical disk technology market in early 1989 included WORM (Write Once Read Many) erasable optical, compact disk-video, interactive videodisk, compact disk-interactive, interactive compact videodisk, Digital Video Interactive, and optical memory card,[20] CD-ROM is the most familiar optical disk technology currently on the market. Introduced in 1985 by the Library Corporation for their BiblioFile Catalog Production, CD-ROM initially had a limitation which has since been overcome: the high cost of updating and storage of text-only material. CD-ROM developments have incorporated graphics, pictures, audio capabilities and artificial intelligence.[21] Each disk stores from 5,000 to 200,000 pages.

A growing number of reference tools and indexes are offered in the CD-ROM format. CD-ROM products are used in cataloging and retrospective conversion, and the format is used for retrospective case law. ADONIS, the trial document delivery service, supplies over 200 biomedical journals published between 1987 and 1988 on CD-ROM.[22] Yet another CD-ROM application is the CD-PAC developed by the Tacoma Public Library. The CD-ROM public-access catalog "interfaces to another computer system which supports a circulation system. The concept of a CD-PAC-to-circulation system linkage is simple: off-load the searching to the PC to minimize the load on the circulation system, and limit the circulation system for status information on demand."[23]

CD-ROM material is retrieved on a microcomputer workstation with a CD-ROM drive attached. Since micros have become an integral part of every day life, users accept the convenience offered by CD-ROM.

Because the material is in a computer drive, storage space requirements are minimal, eliminating floor loading and collection maintenance concerns and recovering substantial space.

CD-ROM is automated information without the need for telephone lines and the expenses associated with online retrieval. It is available as needed, whenever the library is open and the electricity available. CD-ROM databases simulate on-line searching with their keyword indexes.

The projected disadvantages are in the initial equipment costs, equipment maintenance costs, security of the disks, and an accurate prediction of an adequate number of workstations. Standards for drives, disks, and interfaces are emerging.

TECHNOLOGY AND RESOURCE SHARING

The traditional concept of interlibrary loan has evolved into a concept of designed resource sharing. Resource sharing signifies formal agreements, usually as a membership or formal partnership, among libraries cooperating on purchasing, storing, weeding and/or preserving of collections in addition to traditional interlibrary loan activity. It also predicates a technological underpinning to support the program, be it an online system containing holdings information with capabilities for transmitting traditional interlibrary loan requests, or other support equipment such a fax machines, scanners/digitizers, plus dial-access capability for downloading files of data. Technology is a tool for supporting innovative resource-sharing programs.

Norman A. Fink and Richard Boivin describe a very sophisticated resource sharing program supported by an integrated on-line system. "MultiLIS Book Exchange Process: A 'Shuttle' Approach to Collection Development" describes a Canadian regional library system designed to support public libraries in communities of less than 5,000 people. In many ways, the system functions as a regional lending library. "Local libraries are encouraged to acquire mostly reference materials, bestsellers, and very popular books, while the regional lending library supplements the local collection in fiction and nonfiction materials with a diversified collection of some 40,000 to 50,000 titles, generally available in three to six copies. The work of the regional lending library primarily consists of acquiring resources and controlling the exchange of materials among libraries. Essentially, it comprises the management of multiple library collections and the production of bibliographic tools."

MultiLIS accomplishes the materials exchange, and the authors describe it as "very comprehensive integrated system which allows networking between local and regional libraries."[24] Each library's basic collection is also exchanged periodically. While the goal is to maximize the use of library materials, the authors note strong storage implications.

Cooperative resource sharing has received increased attention as purchasing power declines, publishing output grows, telefacsimile and computer-assisted interlibrary loan programs and delivery systems enhance information exchange, and patrons seek a broader range of materials. However, Dick Dougherty states, "The principal objective of a shared collection/shared resources program should be to increase access to specialized materials or to materials users request which are not available in local collections. . .we miss the point when we talk about resource sharing as a substitute for local ownership. The goal of shared collection development programs ought to be to provide access to publications that individual libraries are currently unable to purchase. . . ."[25]

Cooperative storage programs and last-copy retention agreements will have the greatest impact on local library-collection space needs. With the former, on-site collection growth space may be retrieved, but there will be a cost, either direct or indirect, to participate in the remote storage program. The last-copy retention program will alter weeding options and may determine the amount of local growth space required.

Another technological development is the emergence of the "scholar workstation." Michael Bauer envisions researchers who have access to regional and national libraries and the ability to arrange interlibrary loan requests from their offices. With the workstation, researchers can download from online resources and search specialized databases, processing and manipulating a variety of information resources at the local workstation.[26] The workstation is not just a microcomputer, but an environment containing enhanced interfaces with pointing devices and applications such as hypertext, with windowing capabilities to deal with a multiple work functions on the same screen. The space implications of this scenario are astounding: libraries may provide on-line access to information sources rather than retaining extensive holdings on-site.

Developing technologies and new technological applications will continue to change the use of traditional library space. For example, an online catalog or CD-ROM catalog frees some of the area formerly committed to a card catalog and may provide a net gain in square footage. The introduction of online acquisitions systems reduces the amount of space required for extensive paper files and the associated record keeping. The use of word processors and microcomputers, in theory at least, enables librarians to reduce the space committed to file cabinets.

THE "BOOK" OF THE FUTURE?

Katie Blake describes "The Electronic Book,"[27] which she believes will supersede the printed book. One version, the Smart Book, consists of a reader unit about the size of textbook with a removable "bookpack." The reader unit has a liquid crystal display, (with a portrait-style screen option), user control buttons, and flip-down tilt stand. The "bookpack," which contains the text, is about the size of a credit card. At present, it holds one megabyte of ROM using conventional microcomputer chips, held in the pack by a proprietary compressed format. (The prototype bookpack is text-only at present because of the significant storage space requirements for pictures and other graphics).

In the early stages, Blake foresees applications to reference materials like directories, dictionaries, and so forth. She notes that distribution of books through the mail would be extraordinarily easy and inexpensive. Data could also be downloaded over the phone lines. The space-saving implications are enormous.

REFERENCES

1. Michael Gorman, "Movable Compact Shelving: The Current Answer," *Library Hi Tech*, 5 (Issue 20, Winter 1987): 26.
2. Leslie R. Morris and Frank M. Webster, "Public Use of Compact Shelving" *Collection Management*, 10 (1988): 121-30.
3. Martin H. Collier, "Sixth Stack Addition" *Library Journal*, 107 (December 1, 1982): 2235-7.
4. For a brief and easily understood discussion about floor loading, read David H. Eyman's "Floor Loading Problems in Academic Libraries" *Library Administration and Management*, 1 (June 1987) 3: 97-9. Eyman reviews floor loading requirements for standard stacks, microforms, and office space, applicable to all types of libraries contemplating re-use of existing space.
5. Charles R. Smith provides a checklist for writing compact shelving specifications and a list of vendors in "Compact Shelving Specifications" *Library Administration and Management*, 1 (June 1987) 3: 94-5.
6. Thomas A. Bourke, "Mega Microforms: Ambitious New Publication Projects for Scholarly Research" *American Libraries*, 18 (March 1987): 184-7.
7. Stephen R. Salmon, "Economics of Regional Storage Facilities" speech delivered at the American Library Association Annual Conference, Dallas, 1979.
8. Alice Harrison Bahr, *Microforms: The Librarian's View, 1978-1979* (White Plains, N.Y.: Knowledge Industries Publications): 53-7.
9. Two excellent guides on microforms management are *Developing Microform Reading Facilities* (Richard W. Boss with Deborah Raikes, Westport, Conn.: Microform Review, Inc., 1981) and *Microforms in Libraries: A Manual for Evaluation and Management*, Francis Spreitzer, Editor, (Chicago: American Library Association, 1985); both include space planning chapters. Articles devoted specifically to aspects of the microforms physical environment are William K. Ach, "Lighting in Microtext Rooms" *Microform Review*, vol. 14, no. 3 (Summer 1985) 171-3: and Arthur C. Tannenbaum, "Microform Room Environments: The External Factors" in *The Serials Librarian*, 5 (Spring 1981): 25-34.
10. Valerie Jackson Feinman, "Store It, But Don't Ignore It" *The Serials Librarian* 10 (Fall 1985/Winter 1986): 201-10.
11. John Kountz, "Industrial Storage Technology Applied to Library Requirements" *Library Hi Tech*, 5 (Issue 20, Winter 1987): 13-22.
12. "Storage Facility: Final Report" *ARL SPEC Kit 97*, Building Renovation in ARL Libraries (Washington, D.C.: Association of Research Libraries, Office of Management Studies, September 1983): 33.
13. *University of California Libraries: A Plan for Development, 1978-1988* (Berkeley: University of California Office of the Executive Director of University-Wide Library Planning, 1977): 48.
14. John J. Boll, "To Grow or Not to Grow" *LJ Special Report #15* (New York: R. R. Bowker, 1980): 16.

15. Ibid.:17.
16. Richard Trueswell, *Analysis of Library User Circulation Requirements—Final Report*, NSF Grant #435 (Washington, D.C.: Government Printing Office, 1968).
17. Allan Kent et al., *Use of Library Materials; The University of Pittsburgh Study* (New York: M. Dekker, 1979).
18. F. W. Lancaster, "Obsolescence, Weeding, and the Utilization of Space" *Wilson Library Bulletin*, 62 (May 1988): 47-9.
19. Pamela Q. J. Andre, "Optical Disc Applications in Libraries" *Library Trends*, 37 (Winter 1989): 326.
20. "Special Issue: 1989 Buyer's Guide and Consultant Directory" *Optical Information Systems*, 8 (November-December 1988): vi.
21. Nancy Harrison and Brower Murphy, "Multisensory Public Access Catalogs on CD-ROM" *Library Hi Tech*, 5 (Issue 19, Fall 1987): 77-80.
22. Barrie T. Stern and Robert M. Campbell, "ADONIS: Delivering Journal Articles on CD-ROM (Part I)" *CD-ROM Librarian*, 4 (February 1989): 9-13.
23. Kevin Hegarty, "The Compact Disk-Circulation System Interface at the Tacoma Public Library: Beyond Stand-Alone CD-ROM" *Library Hi Tech*, 6 (Issue 23, 1988): 103.
24. Norman A. Fink and Richard Boivin, "MultiLIS Book Exchange Process: A 'Shuttle' Approach to Collection Development" *Library Hi Tech*, 6 (Issue 23, 1988): 64, 70.
25. Richard M. Dougherty, "A Conceptual Framework for Organizing Resource Sharing and Shared Collection Development Programs" *The Journal of Academic Librarianship*, 14 (November 1988): 291.
26. Michael Bauer, "The Emerging Role of Workstations in the Library Environment" *Library Hi Tech*, 6 (Issue 24, 1988): 37-46.
27. Katie Blake, "The Electronic Book" *Library Hi Tech*, 6 (Issue 21, 1988): 7-11.

4 ASSESSING FACILITIES

Accurately assessing the building and equipment is as important to the space planning process as measuring the collection and the collection housing. Each facility has characteristics that will affect how the space is used and the library resources allocated. While library personnel cannot provide the same degree of specificity in a building assessment as engineers, architects, and construction professionals, they must be aware of the characteristics of their building. They can use this knowledge for effective space planning, in conjunction with these professionals.

Before we begin the discussion about the building assessment, we are assuming that the library facility has already been assessed for asbestos and that if asbestos is present, a control plan or action plan has been devised. Under the 1986 Asbestos Hazard Emergency Response Act (AHERA) and the AHERA Regulation published in the Federal Register on October 30, 1987, local education agencies are required to take comprehensive action about this problem.

It can affect the safety of all building users. If an assessment has not already been conducted, it should be done before any building renovation occurs. Consulting firms specialize in asbestos surveys and assessments as well as asbestos management and abatement programs.

Asbestos is usually found when embarking on a remodeling project, as was the case with the Connersville Senior High School Library in Connersville, Indiana, and the Main Library of the Suburban Library System in Hinsdale, Illinois.[1] In Hinsdale, the asbestos was found in the 1951 building when the Board investigated replacing the ceiling.

ASSESSING THE BUILDING

FLOOR PLANS

The first step in examining a building for space planning is to acquire—and understand—a recent, accurate floor plan, architectural drawing, or blueprint. Plans that are essential for evaluation of the building include accurate markings of permanent physical characteristics: walls (especially load-bearing walls), pillars, floors, stairwells, elevators, and windows. Since plans and blueprints do not always contain all of the information required, it might be necessary to look at several plans of the same room to glean all of the facts needed.

During construction or renovation, each subcontractor will have a set of plans that details the work to be done in his or her area of specialization. Separate plans are drawn up for plumbing, wiring, furniture layouts, the air handling system, landscaping, carpentry, walls, windows, and such special equipment installations as compact shelving or an internal computer network.

Building plans are not always readily available. Sources for locating the floor plans and old construction drawings are scattered throughout the organization and the community:

- The contractor who did the last rehab or the institutional maintenance department may have a set of "shop drawings," drawings used on-site by the plumber, carpenter, or electrician.
- The organizational archives may contain the original construction plans.
- If local public library was built through the guidance of the county engineer, the engineer's office should have the plans on file.
- Building inspectors occasionally keep files of plans for public buildings.
- Plans may be found from a reorganization which took place ten years ago, but not last year's reorganization. Or the only plans available may be those used to propose a new configuration which was never implemented.

If the library is undergoing construction or renovation for the reorganization, floor plans detailing work underway or planned will be available on site from the clerk of the works. The condition and accuracy of these plans will vary. If a contractor or an architect is working on the job, he or she will be able to help interpret the plans or draw new ones if needed.

The library space planner and the staff need to verify that, once located, the plans in hand contain accurate measurements. Verification is done by measuring, drawing, and noting modifications and changes. Measure and double-check the plans for accuracy of the location of permanent features before furniture and collection layouts are attempted.

To check the plans, pace off room sizes, door placements, columns, windows, and walls. If the measures gained in the pacing-off process don't match the measures on the floor plans, use tape measures and measure again. If they are still different, change the floor plans to reflect reality. We know of one library reorganization that had to be changed during the actual move because the layouts were done on plans from the organization's physical plant department. Due to a change during construction, the windows varied at least one foot from the blueprint designations.

When plans are not available, they will have to be drawn. Start a plan by outlining the permanent features of the library building, using graph paper and an architect's rule or one of the CAD programs available, such as ROOMER 2[2]. However, if using a CAD program, be sure to allow enough time to learn the program and test it before committing to this format. Sometimes the printers and plotters available will not support the application; other times the memory available on the PC useful for spreadsheets and word processing will be inadequate for a CAD program.

If you are hand drawing the plans, use a scale of at least $1/4'' = 1'$ because a smaller scale is very hard to work with, leading to errors. Consider hiring a draftsperson or an architect when professionally drawn plans are not available. Basic books on blueprint reading should be consulted before any plans are drawn or revised for an explanation of the standard symbols and basic rules.[3]

Make working copies of the accurate plans in order to record the information gathered when assessing the building and the furnishings. A final master copy, reflecting all notations, becomes a part of the space data file. Several copies of the final plan are also necessary for the workers and for the files.

A number of elements must be considered when assessing a building. The floors, floor loading capacity, floor coverings, walls, windows, columns, wiring, and lighting are features that control space allocation within a building. Each of these features is discussed in some detail below from the perspective of library space planning. Architects, building consultants, and other professionals can provide more detailed information as required.

FLOORS

Evaluate the general condition of the floors, their composition, load-bearing capacity, and covering for inclusion in the space data file. The file should also contain information about the structural design of the building as well as the floor supports. These features often determine reallocation options.

Factors to consider in evaluation include:

- Are the floors smooth and level? Take a carpenter's level and place it at several different locations on the floor. If the floor is uneven, mark the plans to show the direction of the

FIGURES 1 AND 2

The layout in Figure 1, a drawing of the main floor of a court library, created erroneous conclusions about available shelving and user space because it was not drawn to scale. The layout in Figure 2 is drawn to scale and accurately represents what will fit into the first floor of this library. Note the flight of stairs, which limits the amount of space.

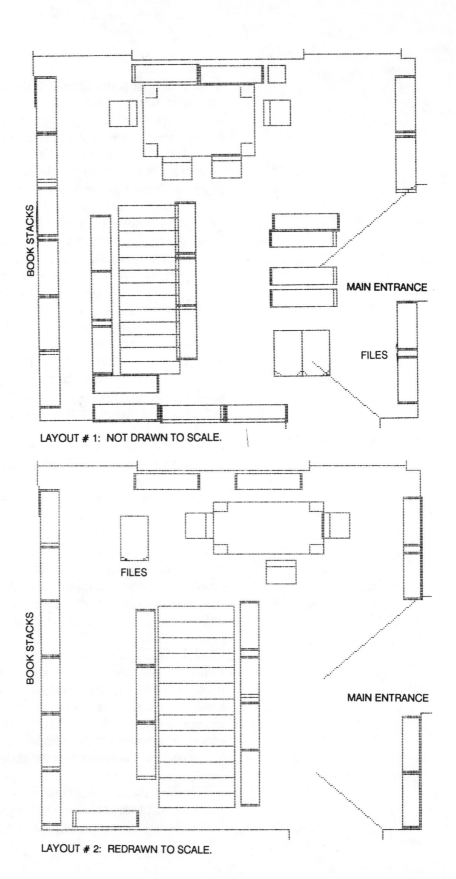

LAYOUT # 1: NOT DRAWN TO SCALE.

LAYOUT # 2: REDRAWN TO SCALE.

slant or the location of the bulge or bubble. Many buildings settle over time and have slightly uneven floors, which affect the placement of furniture.

- Wavy floors lead to balancing problems for shelves, tables, carrels, and equipment. Investigate the cause of a wavy floor, especially if the waves are of some magnitude. Improper floor loading also leads to waves in the floors.
- Termites are not unheard-of. If they've been there a while, they may have weakened the structure.
- Individual tiles can cause a problem. Floors may wave and buckle and the edges of the tiles stick up. Worn tiles are not only unsightly, but are also prone to tearing when furniture and equipment are moved; they also prevent sliding a piece of furniture or equipment across the floor. Sometimes loose joints in the tiles indicate a water problem. Be sure that the leak has been repaired.

WEIGHT LOADING

"Following the discovery of a sagging floor in the Clarissa, Minnesota, High School, officials moved the library and discontinued use of classrooms on the top floor." After reading that a floor in a Lanesboro, Minnesota, high school collapsed, The school superintendent of Clarissa ordered an inspection that was carried out by structural engineers.[4]

Most librarians are aware of floor loading issues, this being one thing which usually gets a serious response from even the most obtuse administrator. Every librarian can probably cite at least one overcrowded library with materials resting on an inadequate support system. Professional help from a structural engineer will be required before the space allocation decisions are made if there is no documentation in the library about the floor loading capacity.

If the floor is the problem, one indication of trouble will appear during the floor assessment. The current arrangement of the furniture and equipment could be creating a precollapse condition, where the floors are waving and shifting in response to the load.

Discussions of floor loading differentiate between live and dead loads. A dead load does not move and remains constant over a period of time. Books, microform cabinets, storage cabinets, and office furnishings constitute live loads. In the United States, buildings constructed since World War II have a typical floor capacity of 50 to 80 pounds per square foot, adequate for offices but inadequate for fully loaded cabinets and library books. For library purposes, the weight of such objects as shelving, files (card catalogs and office files), and furnishings (not including compact shelving) should not exceed 150 pounds per square foot, averaged across the floor.[5]

If the budget is not sufficient to pay for a consultation by a structural engineer or architect, talk to people in the maintenance department and all others who may have been involved in the building's construction. If the library is located in a building which was once a firehouse or a school, look at the papers and pictures from earlier occupants for clues to the original use of the space and the possible floor-loading configurations. Look through source materials on architecture and building construction for the period in which the structure was built. Record the information in the space data file and use it when drawing the layouts.

CARPETING

Carpeting has a significant impact on the allocation of space within the library and on the ability of the library staff to carry out space reorganization activities. In fact, one reason for a move may be the excessive wear on a carpet area and a need to change the traffic flow as an inexpensive alternative to replacing the carpeting. Another reason can be the difficulty in pushing book trucks over deep pile carpeting.

Note the characteristics of the carpeting when assessing the floors. Even the most sturdy commercial grade of carpeting eventually wears out, developing holes and showing lumps and protruding threads.

Most carpet is machine produced in either 12' or 15' widths, constructed by punching long threads into a backing. When this method is used, a pulled thread can make a new seam in the length of the carpet, causing a weak area in the carpeting. Pulled threads make moves slower, create safety problems, and may cause unsightly situations mandating a revision in an already revised floor plan.

Weak areas are in the carpet from the start since seams are inevitable in a carpet's installation. Mark the location of the seams on the floor plan. When designing the space plan, do not plan heavy traffic areas where the carpet seams are located. Protect seams from heavy traffic during a move by temporarily covering them with tape.

Mark uncarpeted floor areas on the plan. In some buildings, carpeting is installed in limited locations, used only to define the use of that space. This practice places limitations on the future uses of the space. In general, machinery is often placed in noncarpeted areas because the floor area is easier to clean and tile does not generate static electricity. As technological demands grow and the needs of the library change, the location of the machinery and equipment will change.

Some equipment is sensitive to static electricity, while other machines use fluid or fine powder or require frequent cleaning with fluids. The type of equipment will determine what can be located on which carpeted areas. For example, static electricity can damage a microcomputer's hard disk, so if the microcomputer is stationary, as opposed to a laptop, consider a location where static is minimal or purchase an anti-static mat.

Carpeting is installed using one of three common techniques: gluing to the floor, stretching and hooking to tack boards, or a combination of both. Each method has its own problems. Glue may have been applied unevenly; heat and humidity in the building can cause it to dry out or otherwise change its consistency. Removing glue from the floor if the area is not to be recarpeted is a challenge. Tack board installations can come loose, causing waves and ripples in the carpet. Removal of tackboard will leave large holes in the floor. If the alternative floor plan hinges on carpet removal, allocate additional funds for complications that may arise. Prepare for this by noting the method of carpet installation on the floor plans or in notes attached to the plans.

Carpet tiles are frequently used in high-traffic areas to enable replacement of worn sections as opposed to the whole area. Drawbacks of this option include:

- The replaced tile will look different from those surrounding it because of routine wear on all of the tiles.
- Color and pattern require special attention because of future replacements.
- Installation must be perfect, as the tile installation is, basically, a large collection of seams.

When walls are constructed over carpeting, waves and lumps occur if the floor underneath the wall is not even or if the carpet is not stretched enough and fastened firmly. Usually, by the time this problem becomes apparent, the walls are constructed and the lighting and wiring are in place. The only way to repair the waves is to cut the carpet and install additional tackboard and restretch all of the carpet; molding will usually have to be moved. The time and effort factored into each of the repair items impacts the timing of the space plan implementation.

The quality, condition, method of installation, and location of the carpet have been noted. One major consideration remains in the carpet assessment: the color and type. Different types of carpet are often separated by different patterns and colors. The quality of the carpet is determined by where it is to be used. Executive offices often have plush carpeting while the higher-traffic areas are carpeted with sturdy commercial grade. Note each of these areas on a floor plan. Locating high-traffic functions on cheap carpet or high-pile carpet will mandate another move or replacement of the carpet in a comparatively short time.

A carpet pattern of wavy stripes and lines or geometric patterns can confuse patrons and staff when stacks and ranges clash with the pattern. If is not be possible to change the carpeting, the space configuration for the library will have to be designed around it.

WALLS

Space data files should include details about the current and anticipated use of walls and wall space. The composition of the walls defines what can be fastened to them. Many libraries use wall space to hang bulletin boards, shelving, videotape display units, and framed art prints. However, some walls were not constructed for holding a bulletin board, much less shelving. Some walls are designed to be moved; others are load bearing or house the building's heating and wiring and cannot be moved without expensive renovation. Still other walls are unsuited for shelving or hanging the print collection because of permanent attachments or construction characteristics.

The type of wall composition determines the method used for supporting the shelves, bookcases, or other wall-hung items. Many buildings constructed before World War II have press-board interior walls. Press-board and sheet-rock require special screws or molybolts in order to attach an angle brace to a shelf unit for hanging it on a wall; even with this, the shelving will have a limited load capacity.

Attaching items to masonry or brick walls also requires special hardware and drill bits. If a library was designed with one or more interior walls made of decorative stone or cedar-shakes, this should be noted (with dimensions) on the floor plans, since nothing can be fastened to these walls.

Studs provide locations for fastening heavy items to a wall otherwise unable to support the item. They are also used for carrying the main wiring and the phone lines, and determine the heating and ventilating system configuration.

Locate studs by using a magnet to find the nails that hold the walls to the studs. Once a couple of nails are found, a regular pattern will emerge: most studs are either 12″ or 18″ on center. This means that the center of one stud is exactly 12″ or 18″ from the center of the next. Check each wall; do not assume the pattern will be consistent throughout the building. Indicate stud locations on the floor plan.

Examine the wall heights. Public-use areas should have 10′ high ceilings, while 8′ is satisfactory in office areas. Energy use is affected by wall height and thickness. A room with 50′ ceilings will cost more to heat and cool than one with 8′ ceilings. Noise level will be greater in a high-ceiling room because of the echo effect. Rooms with drop ceilings are deceptive; there can be less than 8′ between floor and ceiling. Shelving options are limited with ceilings lower than 8′; standard shelving cannot fit, and the lighting may cause stressful glare. The canopy shelf may have to be eliminated in rooms with low ceilings, leaving no shield for the books and allowing dust and debris to gather on the materials. Conversely, of course, the exceptionally high ceiling or atrium may contain enough space for a second tier of stacks.

Windows, fire extinguishers, heating or ventilating equipment, alarm boxes, public pay phones, and electrical panels affect the optional space available on each wall. Mark the location of each of these on the floor plan.

WINDOWS
Window locations may affect planned locations for more wall-hung shelving, in addition to affecting lighting and heating requirements. In the space data file, include information on windows: locations, measurements, compositions, treatments, and constraints. Record whether and how the windows open. The glass can be single-thickness, drafty, and delicate; beveled and very thick; opaque and threaded with chicken wire so it cannot break. Some "glass" windows are actually synthetic.

In modern buildings, non-glare glass is used to shield the staff and materials from too much light, while theoretically allowing enough light to enter. However, we know of at least one library which experienced afternoon glare after the non-glare glass was installed. When presented with this problem, the architect and the organization's administration pointed out the manufacturer claimed that glare was not possible. The architect suggested relocating all items in the path of the sun.

Clear glass windows may add more heat and light to an area than the equipment or people can tolerate. In fact, a large section of the library may have a limited use because of window treatment. Sun shining directly onto carpets and upholstery fades and rots fibers, ages and fades books, and ages and may warp non print materials. Check areas at different times during the day and mark any possible problem areas on the floor plan in the space data file. Consider monitoring the temperature and humidity of particularly questionable areas for at least one month.

COLUMNS, PILLARS, AND OTHER STRUCTURAL SUPPORTS

The columns and pillars in a library may provide structural support, serve a decorative purpose, carry the wiring and air handling systems, or some combination of the three. Again, the location of the actual structure must be double checked on the floor plan by comparing measurements. Be sure to determine the function of each column. A decorative column may be easily moved, while the one handling the wiring is a potential source of additional electrical power.

Columns may vary in size and shape within a room. Remodeled buildings often contain several variations. Libraries constructed before the advent of equipment requiring electricity, such as microform machines, frequently have columns added solely to carry needed wiring for electricity and telephones. Library buildings also contain decorative columns, which offer more options to the space planner than do columns with a specific purpose. Decorative columns can be removed, hollowed out, wired, and refinished as the library needs dictate.

WIRING, ELECTRICAL POWER, AND LIGHTING

Electrical power affects the reorganization options available to a space planner and has the potential to create a nightmare for library operations. The amount of power coming into the building, the amount available to the library, and the load on each line is of prime importance. The information about the electrical power in the space data file includes drawings of circuits; locations of switches, plugs, and outlets; the capacity of each line; and the lighting configuration.

Note the locations of any track lighting, and built-in spotlights, as well as "regular" lighting arrangements. They will make a difference in the way the library space is allocated. Lighting is particularly important in open-stack areas, where it is necessary to read without glare, in carrels or reading-study locations, in office work, and in using computers.[6]

Redistribution of power and better use of existing lighting are ever-present goals of any space reorganization. The space planner requires expert advice, preferably in writing, about adding another line to the existing power sources. Library buildings undergoing

FIGURES 3, 4, AND 5

The plans for the library in Figure 3 were drawn to permit the ceiling lighting to fall between the open ranges of shelves. This configuration would have made future collection moves almost impossible. The revised layout, Figure 4, provides more flexibility as well as better lighting. Lighting affected the decision to move ranges in Design Alternative #3 Figure 5 (page 86).

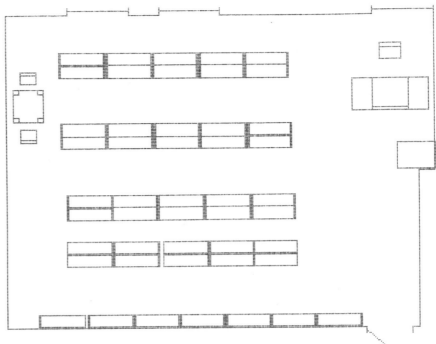

Figure 3. Stacks are lined up so ceiling lighting is between the aisles parallel to the ranges.

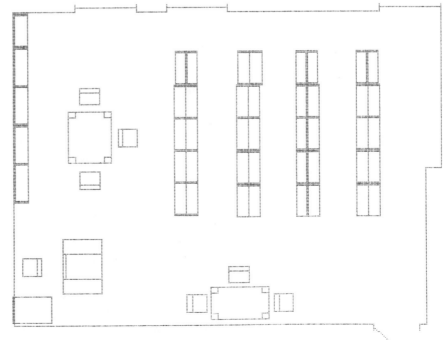

Figure 4. Stacks are lined up so lighting in perpendicular to the ranges.

DESIGN ALTERNATIVE #3

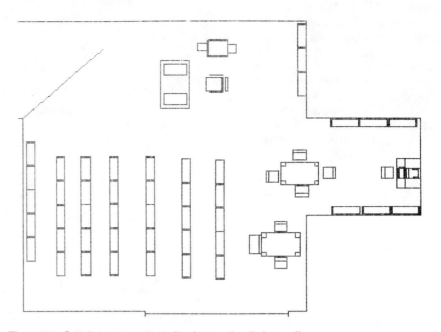

Figure 5. Stacks are perpendicular to the lights; all aisles are visible from the desk.

renovation should be given as many new lines and outlets as possible.

A perverse rule of thumb: wherever a piece of equipment will best fit, power will be inadequate. A corollary to that rule: when a manual operation is automated, the specifications for the product will require that it operate on a dedicated line—an electrical line which has no other appliances or outlets sharing the power source. When the dedicated line requirement is ignored, a service company may refuse to repair or replace the equipment, assuming the damage was caused be inadequate power.

Electrical power was discussed as far back as 1927. In his article, "Library Planning," Edward Tilton suggested that libraries with permanently placed stacks make provision for an electrical outlet at the end of each range.[7] Outlets at the end of each stack section might be a good option, but if all are tied into the same circuit, power outages may occur during normal operations. The strip outlet, a wire along a wall with a continuous strip of outlets attached to it, offers flexibility but does not solve the problem of too many items plugged into one circuit. Especially as more CRT's and pc's are added to libraries, the issue of adequate electrical power assumes increasing importance.[8]

In order to determine the amount of electricity on a circuit or line, divide watts by volts to arrive at the amps. Usually, an instruction book or plate on the equipment will tell you the wattage. Add wattages of equipment most likely to be on at the same time to see if the circuit has more than 2,200 for a 220 line or 1,650 for probability of blowing circuits when all pieces are in operation. If you must order extension cords because of inadequate outlets, try to get cords with a number below 16. The lower numbers carry more electricity.

The essential measuring tool for electrical power is the number of amps coming into the building and the number available on each circuit. For example, a photocopy machine may draw two to three amps when the "print" button is pushed. When this is combined with the three to four amps needed to keep the labeling machine running, and the one to two amps for the typewriter, and the two to three for the air conditioner, the next person to use the electric pencil sharpener may cause a power failure. This failure will cause the circuit breaker to snap. Electrical circuits have a protective attachment in the wiring that will cause the circuit to shut off when overloaded. If the circuits do not shut off in time, a fire can begin.

Wisely allocating power prevents fires and service interruptions which can damage equipment. The damage can be as minor as a lost line in a letter produced on a word processor or as significant as the loss of several transactions in the circulation system. These losses can be alleviated if the assessment process produces a good picture of the library's power supply and its allocation. When the needs and the existing resources are defined, the library space planner will have the information required to allocate electrical power and to avoid overloading circuits and lines.

Existing lighting and electrical allocation can be determined by testing each outlet and switch. First, turn on all the lights in the library. Then, shut off one of the circuits on the library powerboard and mark the lights affected by that circuit on the floor plan. Work with an electric light on a cord to test outlets, including those which normally handle equipment. Go from outlet to outlet and mark the circuits on the plan. Testing each switch and outlet will give you a clear picture of the electrical circuitry in the building.

Assessment of library electrical requirements and reallocation of existing resources within a library will invariably involve the use of extension cords during and following the project. Before ordering these cords, determine the appropriate size by using Figure 6 and the advice of an electrician.[9]

The cord numbers refer to thickness, which also determines the ability to carry the electrical current. Too many pieces of equip-

FIGURE 6. GAUGE OF EXTENSION CORDS

	Up to 25'	Up to 50'	Up to 100'
To 7 Amp	No. 18	No. 16	No. 14
7-10 Amp	No. 16	No. 14	No. 12
10-15 Amp	No. 14	No. 12	No. 10

ment on the same cord, or a cord that is too thin, will cause the cord to overheat and could cause a fire. The longer the cord, the farther it has to carry the current, and so it should be thicker. Thinner cords have a drop in power over a distance.

Some pieces of equipment require 220 wiring. For these pieces of equipment, note the source of the electrical line and its location. Moving a piece of equipment requiring 220 when the library has only one 220 line will require an expensive line change. Most newer machines operate without special lines or 220, but many require special plugs with a ground built in. Grounds are important because they prevent the destruction of equipment and machinery during power surges and drops. In an older building, this may entail using adapters when equipment is moved. Protection from power fluctuations is important.

When dealing with electricity, expect problems and unanticipated situations. For instance, use of power tools during a move will draw upon electrical resources. The use of an elevator, a conveyer belt, or a book cleaner will draw on and redistribute power during the move and could affect ongoing operations.

FURNITURE

Perhaps the space planner has at his or her fingertips a complete and up-to-date inventory of the furniture. In most situations, this is not the case. Furniture is often neglected or taken for granted in library operations. Take stock of the library's furniture and its condition during the measurement and assessment process for the space data file and to build a furnishings inventory database.

The primary objectives of this assessment is to determine if the furniture is in good condition and whether it can be used for its original purpose or is better suited to an alternative function. The process of gathering information about the furniture is the same as that for gathering information about the collection, the collection housing, and the facilities. The furniture is assessed in a logical sequence, item by item, room by room, so the data gathered are complete and retrievable. The detailed descriptions of furnishings are used when bid specifications for moving the library are written. Notes can be kept on a form similar to that in Figure 7. Duplicate the form onto cards for ease of handling. The resulting records become the basis for permanent inventory records. If the organization has a laptop pc, perhaps it could be used in the data gathering process in lieu of or in conjunction with the forms.

The *room* is the room in which the item is located at the time of the review. The *item* is a description of the item such as desk with leg, chair—lounge, steno, side, etc. The *number* can refer to a stock or inventory number if the library keeps equipment records. Each record can list all of one type of furnishing—such as all chairs which are alike—but keep separate records for each room. The information is easier to double-check if the records are maintained this way.

Condition refers to the general condition. If an outside mover is going to be contracted, the condition statement is also used on a

FIGURE 7. FORM FOR ASSESSING FURNISHINGS AND EQUIPMENT

FURNISHINGS AND EQUIPMENT RECORD   ROOM _____

RECORD _____

Item Description _____   Size _____

Inventory Number _____   Quantity _____

Condition (check)   poor _____   good _____   hopeless _____

lock (yes/no)   lock works (yes/no)   key available (yes/no)

needs repair _____

(OVER for special features, obvious problems)

Electrical requirements _____

Use _____   Intended use _____

Comments _____

Initials _____   Date _____

mover's inventory sheet, completed before the move begins. This listing protects both the mover and the client, especially when assessing materials damaged in transit. It is signed by both parties.

The *use* category is provided for those items used for one function although originally intended for another. *Intended use* is an optional category that may be filled in at a later time by the space planner.

CHAIRS

Chairs are easily confused, miscounted, and assigned locations for which they are not suited. During the assessment process, consider all of the chairs in one room by type. The information required about chairs for space decisions includes type, color, style, finish, condition, manufacturer, and present use. When deciding chair utilization, consider if they will survive in their present location for any period of time or if they are best used elsewhere in the space configuration.

Secretarial chairs swivel, roll back and forth, lack arms, are usually upholstered, and have adjustable backs and seats. Those with extra-high backs and arms are executive chairs. Executive chairs come in a variety of finishes: upholstery, plastic, and leather. They usually have arms and may or may not swivel and roll. Also note which chairs are ergonomically designed—that is, have adjustable backs and seat heights.

Side chairs do not swivel or roll. They, too, come in a variety of finishes. When used at study tables, side chairs will show signs of wear on the arms; note this on the form.

Lounge chairs do not function well as side or desk chairs. They have a larger seat area and are often over-stuffed. Leather or vinyl, popular types of upholstery, do not hold up well. The leather and plastics split and get punctured, solid colors are often damaged by pens and pencils and also get filthy very quickly. The condition note for lounge seating will help the library space planner determine if cleaning or replacement is necessary.

DESKS AND WORKSTATIONS

Count all desks and workstations, completing a record for each one. Include information about the number, size, style, manufacturer, color, and condition. Note whether the desks have locks, if the keys are available, and if the locks work. Include this information in the note section of the furniture record.

Single- and double-pedestal are terms associated with office furniture. A single-pedestal desk has drawers on one side only and many do not contain the optional pencil drawer in the center.

Double-pedestal desks have a bank of drawers located on each side. Sometimes the drawers are actually designed as file cabinets. Check the drawer depths, since some desk drawers are only 12" deep, which affects their use.

The standard secretarial desk is single-pedestal and has a leg, or return. The return is the typing stand attached to the desk, perpendicular to the work surface, on the side opposite the drawers. A right-hand return means that the return is a typing leg on the right side of the desk. It is not possible to disassemble and reassemble the desk to change the side of the return. Notes about desks should include whether the desk has a right or left return. In fact, it is not wise to plan the desk layout in a room without this information: a staff member could find himself or herself boxed into a wall unable to open the desk drawers or to fit a chair near the work surface.

Executive desks are usually double-pedestal and have an oversized work surface. In some furniture descriptions, this is called an overhang. If the library has a 60" desk with a 12" overhang, then the desk requires 8' to fit into a room. some executive desks are actually tables with large work surfaces and drawers; others are exceptionally heavy and cannot be easily moved.

The counter-height desk used by reference and circulation often comes in modular form; each of these modules should be counted and recorded separately, with notes about special features, including locked drawers for fine collections, special slots to return books, a lower work surface to house the circulation system, electrical boards for equipment outlets and plugs, display fronts for exhibits and bookshelves, and filler segments to complete a desk.

Other details to be recorded include the color, manufacturer, and method of assembly. Does the desk have swinging gates? Note which side the gates are on. Many large modular units have at least one unit custom-made for the initial installation. Card trays in the modular desk system are often designed to move back and forth on wheels. If such a tray exists, the circulation desk should be examined separately. Was it custom-made for the original installation? Is it divided? Is it damaged? Corner units and end panels should be measured and notations made if they are movable or convertible. Does the woodgrain on all pieces match? Include the answers to all these questions in the notes section about the unit.

One way to determine the condition of a module is to take it apart. A better technique is to inspect the desk modules, marking the locations of the module lines or connecting hooks at points in the construction without actually removing the units. If the module is disassembled into its separate components, a reassembly problem may emerge.

Book drops and accompanying book bins are also part of the library furniture configuration. Most bins come with wheels so they can be pulled out from the drop and moved. The measurements and mobility of the book bins must be noted on the floor plans.

TABLES

Inevitably, if a table is not measured, marked, and placed carefully on a layout, it will be too short, too wide, or about two inches too long for its new location. The multiple uses of tables can cause them to blur in with the other furnishings, making them easily missed during the space evaluation process. Tables are used as microcomputer stations and for microform readers; they can be hidden under display racks, lamps, piles of books and boxes, card catalog units or dictionaries. Make a furniture record for each table, noting its condition, composition, shape, manufacturer, measurement, and seating capacity.

Extra tables are used during a space implementation project. They serve as a station for the handouts, as a temporary circulation area, as a place for workers to return notes, as well as barriers and traffic directors. Each table in use during the project should be marked with its final destination.

Measure index tables and include notes about their construction, size, and such special features as extra legs, removable or add-on dividers, and double widths. An extra-long table can be separated only if the required extra legs are available.

The location of the tables and their relationship to the building walls and pillars must also be noted. Sometimes a table only works well in its location because the floor has the right bumps and waves to keep it stable or it uses a column as its fourth leg. Some of the best library furniture does not have adjustable or leveling legs, so the current location may be the best by default.

SPECIAL PURPOSE FURNITURE

During the space assessment, measure all card catalog cabinets and complete a furniture record for each section. The information to be recorded includes the number of sections or units, finish, type of drawers, manufacturer, number of drawers, whether the drawers have rods, and general condition of the drawers and cabinets.

The expandable, standard card catalog section is generally ordered in units with multiples of eight drawers that fit on a standard base; hence the units are considered stackable. The parts of an expandable section are the base, the drawer units, and the top. However, some card catalog sections are complete, inseparable units, finished as one piece, and a section of drawers cannot be added to them.

The drawers and may or may not be interchangeable among the various catalog units. Test a few to find out which units have interchangeable drawers. The presence of rods for the drawers will determine whether the units can be used in a public-services area. The height of the sections and the base units will determine if the patrons will be able to reach the drawers in the catalog.

Consulting tables, AV equipment trucks, special cabinets designed to hold the 8mm filmloop, tables for picture-book reading, display cases and cabinets for equipment are examples of other special purpose furnishings. Each piece of special furniture should be assessed and notes made about its manufacturer, color, design, dimensions, functions, and location.

Tighter budgets and limited resources mandate creative uses of existing furniture and equipment. When the furnishings are surveyed, part of the record will contain notes about possible makeshift arrangements. Identify alternative uses for both the furnishings and space. For example, if the microfilm readers have been placed in carrels because they will not fit on a table, the assessment may make it possible to find a table that accommodates the readers, thus freeing the carrels for seating. If the receiving area has used a library table for stacking incoming mail, maybe this is the time to get a steel shipping table and return the library table to the user area.

Library furnishings are occasionally on loan to other units in the organization. Display cases and special racks, such as newspaper holders, have a tendency to move from the library to other departments for special occasions or as a trade for something else. Track down and inventory each of these items; it may be necessary to call back the loan.

EQUIPMENT

Increased reliance on nonprint materials and online retrieval has resulted in more equipment. The practice of maintaining a centralized inventory of equipment is now common. It is used not only for service contracts but also for insurance purposes, setting a dollar valuation on the items in the library. An inventory list includes the brand name, serial number, date of purchase, and name of the piece of equipment. One style of equipment-inventory record includes columns for each piece of equipment, indicating the condition of the item and its estimated useful life, for tax purposes. A complete equipment inventory includes all of the items in the library listed either by room or by type of equipment.

The space planner should use the data assessment phase of space planning as an opportunity to update the inventory and to include information for insurance reports or renewal of service contracts. Enter the equipment information onto the same record cards used for furniture. Rolling equipment schedules are used, and these will tell the planner if some of the equipment on hand is scheduled to be replaced in the next year or two.

PHOTOCOPY MACHINES AND COMPUTERS

Photocopy machines and computers have specific requirements that affect location options; moving them often requires separate contracts and structural alterations. In fact, the photocopy company may require a special contract with a specified moving company for moving this equipment. These special conditions and contracts are added to the space data files.

Use the equipment booklets that come with the units to learn the dimensions, wiring requirements, and ventilation requirements. Many books will also contain instructions about moving the item. Ventilation is a serious consideration; too many photocopy machines in one room can generate so much heat that they malfunction. If guidebooks have been lost, call the manufacturer or the company holding the service contract for the item. These companies provide specifications and advice about locations and moving.

In moving a mainframe, remember:

- Work closely with the library systems person in site planning and moving plans.
- Check service contracts and consult with the vendor or manufacturer about machine room requirements for the computer.
- Do not plan to move the machine room without expert advice to ensure that the power is adequate, air conditioning and air conditioning back-up are available, an anti-static floor is installed, and security is satisfactory.

Security for each of these items is important. If they are to be moved and the library is not restricted by equipment service contracts, gather special packing boxes and materials to use in the move. All of these special requirements should be determined before decisions are made about the location of each item and the technique for moving it.

MICROFORM AND AV EQUIPMENT

Count and assess microform and AV equipment much the same way as the photocopy machine and computer equipment. Determine how much equipment there is; lighting and wiring requirements; and if other environmental requirements must be considered. Most AV equipment can be moved by the library staff, but there are exceptions.

Arrangements for moving involves removing light bulbs and glass and protecting delicate circuits and mirrors. If the AV equipment is housed in wet carrels, then the space planner should note the equipment and the carrel as one item and include the dimensions and electrical requirements.

EQUIPMENT FOR THE MOVE

Evaluate the equipment necessary to complete the move. One place to begin is with the booktrucks because so many will be needed. Like tables, booktrucks have a way of blending into a library's operations since they are used for purposes other than holding books—as ersatz AV equipment carriers, plant holders, shelving, and photocopy machine holders.

Several types of booktrucks are on the market, and each is suited to a specific set of circumstances. There are double-shelf, triple-shelf, wood, metal, flat, double-sided and single-sided booktrucks. Within the types, there are wheel variations. The information about the trucks should include details about the wheels: Are they turning wheels on each side? Guide wheels? Is there a spring mechanism which will enable the truck to carry extra weight? The space planner should be aware of any booktrucks which might fall apart in the middle of the move or are in no condition to be used for moving.

Flatbed trucks or dollies are the vehicle of choice when moving boxes. This part of the assessment may involve close cooperation with the plant or maintenance department, from which the library will have to borrow the trucks. The size and condition of availability of these trucks must be determined. If it is possible to borrow them only at a certain time of the year or after a certain time of day, then the space planner may have to alter the arrangements for the move or the conditions of the loan.

MISCELLANEOUS ITEMS

An examination of the library's equipments should include the little things—items necessary for operations that everyone takes for granted:

- Wastebaskets, for example, should be counted and the sizes noted so there are enough to go in the right places in the new arrangement.
- Coat racks are essential pieces of equipment: Do they move? What type are available?
- Do not forget pencil sharpeners. Electric sharpeners must be near an outlet, and wall sharpeners must be mounted in an accessible location.
- Where are the water fountains located?
- What about portable display boards and bulletin boards?
- What about reading lamps?
- Were the dictionary stands counted?
- Literature display racks are another overlooked item.

REFERENCES

1. Jo Ann Mareachen, "Asbestos Removal Steps" *Indiana Media Journal*, 10 (Summer 1988): 19-20.
   Lester Stoffel and Ronald S. Kozlowski, "Asbestos Is Bad News" *Illinois Libraries*, 67 (November 1985): 816-18.
2. *ROOMER 2: Floor Plan and Interior Design Software,* published by Hufnagel Software, 1988 (501 H Main St., Box 747, Clarion, Penn. 16214).
3. For assistance with blueprints consult Donald R. Hooper, *Blueprint Reading Made Easy* (Dreyfus, 1983, rev. ed.) or R. Paul Lightle's *Blueprint Reading and Sketching* (McKnight, 1983).
4. "Sagging Floor Detected: School Library Moved" *School Library Journal*, 32 (August 1986): 13.
5. Aaron Cohen and Elaine Cohen, *Designing and Space Planning for Libraries: A Behavioral Guide* (New York: R. R. Bowker, 1979): 91.
6. Ibid.: 123-53, for a discussion of lighting. Bradley A. Waters and Willis C. Winters, "On the Verge of a Revolution: Current Trends in Library Lighting" (*Library Trends*, 36 (Fall 1987): 327-49) is also very helpful. Philip D. Leighton and David C. Weber also cover lighting in *Planning Academic and Research Library Buildings* (Chicago: American Library Association, 1986): 396-405.)

7. Edward L. Tilton, "Library Planning" *Architectural Forum*, 47 (December 1929): 506.
8. For more information about VDT and PC electrical and data power needs read Bennet J. Price, "Computer Power: Part 1: Distribution of Power (and Communications)" *Library Hi Tech*, 6 (Issue 24, 1988): 91-100.
9. *Reader's Digest Complete Do-It-Yourself Manual* (Pleasantville, N.Y.: Reader's Digest, 1973, 1987): 259.

ADDITIONAL SOURCES

William S. Pierce, *Furnishing the Library Interior* (New York: Marcel Dekker, Inc., 1980) discusses the selection, evaluation and procurement of furniture and equipment used in libraries and includes a chapter on "Interior Appointments and Systems" that evaluates HVAC, lighting, floor coverings, wall coverings, windows, doors, etc. "Planning Aids for New Library Buildings" (HBW Associates, Inc., *Illinois Libraries*, 67, November 1985: 794-810) has guidelines for planning a building project from A to Z and also sections on lighting, floor loading, building energy management, planning for better maintenance, and a checklist for barrier free access. The bibliography is excellent.

Redesign of the work environment for CRTs is currently a hot topic. Before reorganizing and rearranging CRT stations, whether for staff or public use, read at least some of the following relevant studies:

David C. Genaway, "Ergonomics: Environment: Energy: A Brief Primer for Site Preparation" *Technicalities*, 9 (January 1989): 10-13.

Judith L. Bube, "The Application of Ergonomic Principles to Workstations" *Technicalities*, 6 (November 1986): 9-12.

A. Cakir, D. J. Hart and T. F. M. Stewart, *Visual Display Terminals: A Manual Covering Ergonomics, Workplace Design, Health and Safety, Task Organization* (New York: John Wiley and Sons, 1980).

John Vasi, "Staff Furnishings for Libraries" *Library Trends*, 36 (Fall 1987): 377-90.

Lamar Veatch, "Environmental Design of Library Buildings" (*Library Trends*, 36 (Fall 1987): 361-76, is very useful reading when planning new layouts of user space. If certain user behaviors are expected and taken into consideration, proper arrangements will support the expected behaviors.

Fred Dubin, "Mechanical Systems and Libraries" *Library Trends*, 36 (Fall 1987) 351-60 is recommended reading before assessing a building. He covers climate controls, acoustics, air quality, lighting and raised flooring.

5 BUDGETING

The fund-raising issues for major new construction and renovation are adequately discussed in the literature.[1] The initial cost estimate for a project is considerably more extensive than is detailed in this brief discussion. However, the library space planner working on a reorganization, regardless of size, should have an estimate of the cost of the project. This estimate generates a working budget. The fiscal considerations not only can delay a project, but can determine scope and ability to acquire outside assistance, and may change the space alternative selected. A project budget is essential.

The project budget should provide guidance for gathering the financial information about the new use of library space. Standard budgetary objectives include definition of project costs, establishment of a target figure for bids, and provision of a mechanism for evaluating bids or determining whether or not to put the project out to bid.

Fiscal control is a prime budgetary objective in every project. It is essential for a finite project such as planning the rearrangement of a library. Control means "accountability," signifying the procedures that make sure monies are properly expended. These procedures involve maintaining detailed records of the receipt and expenditure of funds as well as identification of variances from estimated costs. Standard fiscal control techniques include requiring more than one signatures on orders, using a third party to check invoices against the expenditures and budget projections, and requiring still another individual "check" signature on invoices after they have been released.

Another fiscal control measure is allocating segments of the budgeted funds to a job timetable and determining a percentage of each part of the budget to be spent at a specific point on the timetable. One way to determine the percentages is through the use of the simplest form of a timetable: when the project is half completed, 50 percent of the funds should be expended. Another way to relate the budgeted funds to the project uses the task costs. Assign estimated expenditures for each task to the period in the timetable when that task will be completed. The task expenditures in each time period are totaled and converted to a percentage of the amount to be expended for the whole project. Regular reports on the status of the expenditures and fiscal commitments are prepared to assess the progress of the project and to determine if the amount of money spent is equal to the amount estimated.

During the project, any variation of expenditures above or below ten percent of the budgeted amount should be investigated and the reasons for the variance defined so there can be no question of misappropriation of funds or inaccurate charges. It may be accurate to have 75 percent of the budget expended when only 25 percent of the project is completed, but the only way to know this is to actually draw up a schedule.

Budgets must be flexible and yet contain the correct level of detail. There are two major decision points in this process: the first is to decide how much money to commit to each subset; the second is to determine if the costs are to be considered operating expenses or capital expenses. Flexibility is required because the figures included in the initial budget are often estimates. Since estimates, by definition, are not exact, a revision of figures during the course of a project will be needed to reflect actual costs. In a flexible budget, lines are created as needed and funds transferred between categories in exceptional or contingency situations, not as part of routine operation. Too much shifting will reduce or eliminate the value of the budget as a guide and projection tool.

A good working budget will include all anticipated project expenditures in the cost calculation before the work begins. The need to move moneys from line to line is then reduced. Establishing

TABLE 1

The working budget in Table 1 is a weekly summary for part of a library renovation project, the move. The allocated amount in column one is the original esti- mate for that phase of the move. A review of the expenditures to date indicated the security costs would run over the estimate since 84% of the allocation was expend- ed and the extra guards had not yet been hired. However, some funds might be available in the shelving category as an extra discount was obtained. One of these budget worksheets is gener- ated each week as the project moves toward completion.

```
BUDGET   LIBRARY MOVE   WEEK #4      date       5/5/89
COMPLETION DATE   '6/6/89


CATEGORY      ALLOCATION   EXP TO DATE   PERCENT   COMMENTS

Personnel
   labor       $1,000        $200          20     measure,boxes
   prof        $6,000        $4,500        75     lib conslt,engineer

Supplies        $500         $400          80     boxes etc purchase

Rental        $2,500          $0           0

Publicity     $1,000         $400          40     radio, printng

Furniture     $4,500        $3,200       71.11    shelving discount

Overhead

   Phones     $3,000        $2,000       66.67    lines, moved
   Electric     $500          $0          0.00    no invoice
   Security    $2,500        $2,100       84.00    system move


Misc
                $600          $15          2.50    parking fees

TOTALS       $21,500       $12,800       59.53
```

cost estimates calls for many hours of work and close cooperation with budget or purchasing offices.

Find out if there is a contract to facilitate purchasing some items. For instance, office supplies such as boxes, paper, markers, and tape are often contract supplies available at special discounts through academic consortia, school districts, and government agencies. When such a contract is available, check the expiration date and be sure that the item listed is exactly what the library needs for the move and that the contract has a clause for price renegotiation. The timing on price changes is often buried in the contract's fine print, and the prices might have changed since the issuing date. Prices obtained from catalogs and purchasing contracts are estimates and should be rechecked with the supplier just before an order is placed. Catalog quotations are not always firm and often involve shipping charges as well as a flat fee.

Contractor estimates are used to determine the probable cost of structural changes. Since consultants and architects also provide estimates of their charges, the space planner does not need to create estimates independently. However, the library literature on consulting provides some guidance. Do not assume a consultant is too expensive until you investigate actual costs. Sometimes the consultant charges for estimates because a great deal of work is involved in developing accurate figures.

A good budget will have an appropriate level of detail. Too much detail will hinder flexibility, slow progress, and confuse the people involved; too little will make the document meaningless. Noting the estimated number of booktrucks to be purchased is important for budget considerations, but the color of the trucks is not. The level of a budget's detail will depend on the requirements of the library purchasing office and the parent institution. But there should be enough detail so the project manager is able to determine, at a glance, what costs are to be incurred. For example, an estimated number of person-hours committed to the job by both hourly workers and salaried employees should be listed; however, it is not necessary to name the individuals.

ORGANIZING THE COSTS

All costs are either operating or capital. Operating costs are the costs for labor, supplies, personnel, and minor equipment—

usually movable equipment. They pass through the accounting cycle in one fiscal year. Capital costs are those incurred to purchase major pieces of equipment and to finance structural alterations. Purchasing new shelves for a building is a capital cost, for instance. Determine the local definitions of operating and capital costs by consulting with the organization or library business office.

There are two methods for determining project costs, the Task Method and the Overall Method. In the Task Method, the costs for the entire project are determined by totaling all of the costs associated with each task in the project. Start the Task Method by setting up one wide sheet of paper divided into three columns (the budget worksheet). The columns organize all the project operations into a budget format which includes all of the project costs. Head one column "Tasks," which will contain a list of tasks to be done for the project. Head the second and third columns "Operating Costs" and "Capital Costs," respectively. The costs associated with each task will be either operating or capital costs and are entered into the appropriate column. Most costs associated with the process of moving are operating costs. This method is easily done on a spreadsheet. Table 2 was created on Lotus 1-2-3.

The task sheet or column shows each job, divided into smaller steps. For instance, the task titled "Move sections of shelving" (I) will have listed below it the headings (A) label the shelved to be dismantled; (B) dismantle the shelves; (C) transport; (D) reconstruct the shelving; (E) create new range-finders for the shelves. The purpose of the exercise is to determine costs for each task; the segments should be small enough to determine expenditures but not so small that funds cannot be delineated.

It is important that the costs be clearly associated with the task and do not spill over into other duties or appear to be connected to the project but unrelated to a single element. If this does happen, assign these costs to a catch-all task named "general." General costs include items such as:

- surveys
- van rental
- temporary modifications to the building for a special ramp
- wood and labor for building book troughs
- small hardware needed for items to be disassembled and reassembled
- special interim telephone lines
- space rental
- additional wiring and use of electricity
- increased use of air conditioners

TABLE 2

```
Task Method of Building an Estimate

Moving the collection
```

TASK	OPERATING	CAPITAL
Move Sections of Shelving		
Label plan and old shelves		
Labor	$90	
Supplies	$10	
Move books from old shelves		
Labor	$1,200	
Boxes	$600	
Dismantle shelves		
Labor	$180	
Hardware	$100	
Transport		
Labor	$700	
Truck rental	$500	
Reassemble		
Labor	$250	
Misc parts	$500	
Total for this task	$4,130	

- publicity
- advertising for help
- printing, mailing, and advertising a bid
- record changes
- creation of shelflists
- site visits
- architect fees
- consultant fees
- rental space for interim operations
- additional keys or new locks

After the tasks and general expenses have been delineated, identify all costs associated with the project as either operating costs or capital costs.

If using the Overall Method, set up columns to represent the *categories* used by the library for budget breakdowns during regular fiscal operations. Again, list the tasks and allocate their associated costs to the proper column. In this method, the figure listed is for the total estimated cost of the task; segments are not included. The most common categories are: supplies, equipment, personnel, utilities, rentals, and telephone; subdivisions do occur within the categories. For example, supplies will often be separated into office and library supplies; telephone will break down into local and long-distance; and equipment will include replacement and new. Budget costs are divided into operating and capital categories *after* the totals for all the tasks are determined.

The budget method selected should be the one the library space planner is most comfortable using and the one best suited to the fiscal condition of the library. When a space project is undertaken and a specific amount of money has been identified for implementation, the Task Method is the best to use because the greater detail enables fine-tuning and adjustments for the specific elements of the project.

OVERLOOKED COSTS

Costs usually forgotten when planning a library move include: extra security, overtime for plant or maintenance personnel, chargebacks for the use of organizational equipment, and rental of space for the interim service or storage location. If the Task Method is used, these costs are usually placed in the general category. Discussed below are additional costs that are often overlooked.

LAYOUTS
Blueprints are needed for the initial planning and for ongoing phases of the reorganization. In addition, drawings and floor plans are reproduced for distribution to workers. Special supplies and an outside expert may be required.

SURVEYS
Conducting surveys to assess the impact of a new service, to determine use patterns, or to define the best allocation of the materials in the library space configuration costs money. Survey costs include office supplies, staff, and computer analysis or charges for data storage. The costs of survey design and adminis-

tration, including duplication, mailing, and follow-up must be included in the budget.

SUPPLIES AND PERSONNEL

Supply and personnel costs are part of all library space projects and often involve hidden or unanticipated expenses. If, for example, the move is to be facilitated by asking patrons to return all materials on a specified date, then who will do the reshelving? Are there enough booktrucks, or should new ones be purchased? What about staff to handle the added circulation records and to send out overdue notices?

There are many other tasks that cost money. Getting items to and from the various locations and ready for use costs money. Buying new boxes to pack books, delivery charges, personnel to assemble them, and a supply of tape for constructing them. Occasionally, a contract with a professional moving company will contain a clause requiring the library to purchase all of the containers used for the move at a predetermined cost. If the plant department is constructing slides or wooden troughs, who pays for the materials and labor? Even if a generous local business supplies liquor boxes for packing books, who will transport the boxes to the library? How? Tape to seal boxes, pens to write on labels, scissors to cut tape, replacement wheels for bookstrucks, padding for elevators, forms for personnel, first-aid kits, wood and nails for on-site temporary construction must all be included in the project budget.

Personnel costs are operating costs and appear both as part of a task and in the "general" budget category. If regular library staff are going to do the move but full library operations are still going to be offered during the project, the cost of hiring people to do the work of the regular staff must be included in the budget.

EQUIPMENT

Rental equipment such as hoists, trucks, extra booktrucks, flatbed trucks, ramps, cranes, telephone systems, and copy machines are sometimes needed. The cost to rent equipment that will support multiple task is a "general" cost. If the equipment is rented for a specific part of the move, then the rental cost is assigned to this task. If the budget is being built using the Overall Method, the rental costs are in their own category. Include the cost to transport the item and any special deposit in the rental figure.

PUBLICITY

Publicity is absolutely essential during a project. Money is required to do a good job: Press releases must be mailed, notices printed and duplicated, advertising purchased, film for photographs purchased, and parties at the end of the job funded. Signs for interim locations and new permanent signs cost money, and when collections are moved and offices relocated, new signs and range-finders are also necessary.

SAFETY

Fire safety regulations may mandate changes in the space configuration and equipment. Different types of fire extinguishers are required for different types of materials; fire saftey regulations dictate the type and contents of extinguishers, exit lighting, and exit paths. Include in the budget the cost to bring the existing system into compliance. Some movers will mandate purchase of special safety clothing and equipment, especially if books are going to be cleaned during the move.

HEATING AND AIR CONDITIONING

Heating and air-conditioning costs change when the use of the facilities changes. These costs are a significant part of library budgets. In the regular operating budget, these costs are based on use during normal hours and for regular library operations. However, use changes when a moving project is underway. The amount of air consumed when studying or reading is quite different from that consumed when moving books and furniture. Even if the library building is small or windows can be opened, expect an increase in the heat and light charges during the project.

If the move takes place in the summer, check the capacity of the air-conditioning system to be certain it will support the added activity. Personnel responsible for the air-conditioning and heating systems can provide detailed use information, as can the customer-service operation at the local power company. If estimates cannot be secured, then build in an increase of one percent over the usual costs for the time period of the move. Some organizations closely monitor these systems, and the variation may lead to a permanent increase in the library's share of the cost. An explanation by way of an entry in the budget can avoid problems in the ongoing library budget process.

Air is circulated and treated only at designated times during the day in buildings with energy-saving systems. The change in use may mandate a change in these conditions for the duration of the move; it can be a costly change. If there is an override system, budget the costs to perform the override as many times as it needs to be done during the life of the project. Also include the cost to reset the system to pre-project levels. If the system needs to be reprogrammed, this cost can be excessive; it may be cheaper to change the hours of the move.

Some buildings can only open when a staff member is assigned to watch the boiler or the air-conditioning compressors; the cost of these individuals' salaries becomes part of the project's budget as well. Occasionally, a flat fee is charged to cover the costs associated with opening or using the building during off-hours.

INSURANCE

Insurance coverage may have to be altered during the implementation of a library space project. Make sure the library has adequate insurance for the people, materials, and facilities during the move. In most institutions, regular staff are covered because the move occurs during the normal operating hours. However, since a staff member whose regular task is to paste pockets or input records could be injured when loading books onto shelves, the policy should be adjusted to cover these unusual staff activities. Also make certain that volunteers and temporary workers are covered for injuries during the move. Of course, anyone driving a vehicle will be the proud possessor of the appropriate drivers license for the job. Be certain the vehicle is insured for the driver.

DAMAGE AND REPLACEMENT COSTS

Put replacement costs in the budget. If 20 office desks are moved any distance, and professional movers are not used, plan on having to repair at least one damaged desk. Library materials, particularly AV equipment, may also have to be replaced. Equipment on the verge of breakdown only needs to be tipped once to break and the move is a likely time for this to occur. Regardless of the method used to move the materials, equipment will fall apart. Books will have to be rebound, relabled, or have torn pages tipped in. Putting materials in garbage bags or unsealed boxes, sliding books down a chute, slamming things into trays, or having teams race to see how much material they can move at one time creates more damage to the materials than anyone intends.

The budgetary figure for damage should be for the short-term repair costs plus a consultant's cost for an analysis of potential long-term damage. A book dropped on its end may not show wear until it starts to circulate. Library conservation experts can provide estimates of the damage and a recovery schedule for the materials; funds may then be committed to purchasing more boxes and providing enough trained staff to move the materials carefully over a longer period of time. Include costs to provide special training sessions on book handling for workers.

RELOCATING LIBRARY EQUIPMENT

Equipment maintenance contracts often contain a clause voiding the contract if the item is moved by other than an "authorized moving agent." Photocopy machine companies are particularly fussy about this and will void maintenance agreements if machines are moved "illegally." Because photocopy companies often have a moving contract with a transport company, the order for moving the equipment must go to the designated moving company through the photocopy company, and the moving companies must move the machine. The cost for this, which should be entered in the budget, will often exceed $200.

Other items such as preprogrammed cash registers, dial-access equipment, coin changers, and media equipment may also require special handling or a special service call for which the library is charged. Dial-access systems purchased during the 1960s and early-generation computer equipment require special care. Often an electrician or a media technician is hired to prepare equipment for a move.

When the move is to be made without the help of experts, put replacement costs of the most breakable part of the equipment into the project budget. For good measure, add the cost of an extra knob, a lens, a bulb, and a service call.

TELECOMMUNICATIONS

The relocation of telephone and data lines is expensive and will have its own entry in the budget. As soon as it is apparent that a telephone or data line will have to be moved, contact the appropriate telephone company.

If the space project involves renovation using an outside contractor, a telephone line may have to be added during the move for the contractor's use. A new telephone line can cost between $50 and $100, and this is usually a cost borne by the library. When a phone is not installed for the contractor, expect extra calls to be placed on the library's telephone because the contractor needs access to a phone, particularly when completing the job depends on the timely arrival of materials, specialized personnel, and subcontractors.

Is the fax machine slated to be moved? Is a dedicated line available at the new site? The TWX machine has been replaced in many libraries, but if it is still in use, arrangements must be made to move the equipment and the line.

COMPUTER TERMINALS

Costs for moving microcomputers may not be large if done by an in-house expert. The real costs may lie in:

- providing additional security devices for the equipment
- new electrical lines or power strips to support the micros and peripherals
- moving or installing communications lines
- and purchasing appropriate furniture, chairs, housing for the peripherals, and anti-static devices for the new locations.

In the budget projections, include packing materials required to move this equipment, since few organizations retain the orignal boxes. Also include a set of tools so the equipment can be moved and re-connected. And plan to clean the micros and peripherals at some point during the move. Be certain to put in the budget whatever is appropriate—a vacuum, key board cleaner, wipes for the screens, and so forth. The need for cleaning depends to some extent on the in-house maintenance program already in place.

Dedicated computer terminals such as OCLC, RLIN, or other local systems need to be moved by special arrangements. Relocation involves coordinating actitivies with the telephone companies and the company providing the service and paying the charges. Since leased terminals are not the property of the library, the cost of moving them will have to be worked out with the company holding the lease and the telephone company.

CELEBRATION

People's natural inclination is to celebrate after the completion of a particularly intense task. Library space projects are no exception. Whether the people doing the move are volunteers, library workers, or outside contractors, plans will be made for a party or other celebrations. Do not expect the staff to bake cookies or cakes. By this point in the project, they are thoroughly sick of the library and its environs. Even if the staff are not directly involved in every step of the move, their lives have been disrupted by the change in the library. Estimate at least $4.00 per worker for libations. Whether it's tea and crumpets, beer and pizza, or coffee and donuts, money is required. If there is to be rededication, include in the budget the invitations, postage and printing costs, mementos, allocation for a special publication, paper goods, and refreshments.

USING BUDGET WORKSHEETS

Worksheets are valuable in routine library operations. Part of the investigation and determination of potential expenses for a space project involves clarification of the library budget in relation to the budget of the parent institution. For example, if the comptroller or mayor or principal or provost or county legislature or school board has been charging a flat percentage of operating costs to the library budget, the space planner can determine what percentage of what budget items is being carried by the library and how the percentage is being determined. One library discovered it was paying all of the telephone costs for an entire building because it used more than 40 percent of the building's phone service. The disparity surfaced when staff was researching charges for an answering machine for use during a move. Ironically, the move was taking place, in part, because the library was thought to be consuming a disproportionate amount of the institutional budget.

HOW TO USE WORKSHEETS

The budget worksheets provide the raw data for subtotaling project tasks. For example, to determine how much money is needed for the first phase of the operation and how much for the last phase, identify tasks associated with each phase and total the figures. The worksheets can also be used to control expenditures. Simply compare the costs listed in each task area with the actual costs.

Assigning costs to tasks can highlight alternative resources for the move and assess their costs—in the process perhaps finding the best way to spend money. For example, one way to move a card catalog is by unloading the drawers, marking them, and moving the shell to another location; another method is to rent a hoist and move the catalog unit as a whole—if it can survive. When the Task Method is used, moving the card catalog is treated as a separate entry, making the costs associated with moving it readily available on the worksheets.

Using the Overall Method, it is easier to reach a grand total, but more time-consuming to identify the implementation alternatives. For instance, personnel costs are recorded in one lump sum, and the listing by task is not available on the final worksheet. Therefore, the entire budget has to be reworked in order to compare the costs of alternatives.

Worksheets are also useful during the process of project request and justification. The degree of sophistication and the amount of detail required for the justification process are defined by the demand of the organization or governing body. When worksheets are thorough and carefully prepared, they can be used as a back-up to answer questions rapidly and accurately.

If the space project is going to increase an operating budget by 15 percent over the estimated amount in a given year, try to negotiate adjustments to the percentage of organizational overhead carried by the library so the budget does not give an inaccurate impression of library expenditures. Some costs routinely allocated on the basis of square footage include heat, air-conditioning, electricity, telephone, insurance, and grounds maintenance.

COSTS OF INACTIVITY

Just as there costs for moving and starting up services, there are costs for not doing so. People do not usually move books, work stations, and equipment without good reason, but attaching a dollar value to the reason is difficult. However, it is possible, and in some instances it may be desirable to compare the cost of doing a project with the cost of not doing it. This comparison is part of the project justification process, not the actual budget.

SERVICES

Rearrangement because of a new service or an increased commitment to automating operations frequently are causes for a space assessment. Use the cost-benefit analysis technique to determine the cost of not having the service. For example, a tight budget may force closing a service point and therefore reduce total library circulation and increase the theft rate. The decision to combine service points increases staff training costs since the staff working the combined service point will have to be trained for several services. Once they are trained, fewer staff will be required for the public services. A cost-benefit analysis is done not just to sell the product to the administration but to help the library relate costs to functions.

Cohen and Cohen describe a basic cost-benefit analysis for the automation of library services.[2] This outline can be used to create a rough estimate and can be adjusted to provide more information by applying the Task Method described earlier. Questions arise as to which costs should be allocated where during the process of a cost-benefit analysis. If it is necessary to go beyond the task breakdown technique, consult several accounting books[3] or bring in a consultant.

COLLECTIONS

Services and operations erode gradually as space allocation problems grow. As shelves get filled, the fact that not enough room remains for all of a library's materials becomes apparent. The problem surfaces in a school or an academic library at the end of the semester, when many books are returned and the shelves cannot hold the materials. The problem slides for a year or two, until it occurs during the academic year as well. Finally, the library has to face the problem and request resources for collection and space reallocation. This is not easy.

In order to define the problem, calculate the cost in staff time to shelve materials in an overcrowded collection. The objective is to determine the extra time involved in reshelving due to the conditions, *not* just the total staff cost to reshelve. This can be determined by taking the amount of time required, per person, to reshelve materials and multiplying it by the hourly salary figure plus 28 percent for fringe benefits. This sum is the hourly personnel cost.

The extra time figure is obtained by multiplying the time it takes to shelve by the number of books or items being shelved in the crowded and the uncrowded collection. The difference in the two amounts is the estimated cost to shelve books in a crowded collection. For example, it may take one hour to shelve 80 books in a library which is not overcrowded. If this library reshelves 100,000 books per year, then it will take 1,250 hours per year to reshelve the normal load. If shelvers are paid $5.00 per hour, the cost to shelve books is $6,250 per year. If the library is overcrowded, it may take one hour to shelve 64 books and a total of 1,562.5 hours to reshelve 100,000 volumes. At the same rate of pay, reshelving in the crowded collection is at least $7,813 per year, an increase of $1,563 per year due to crowding. If there is no count of the items reshelved, assume that all of the items circulated will have to be reshelved and use this figure.

An alternate way of determining basic reshelving figures is to use the "typical week" technique. There is some controversy within the American Library Association about using this concept, but the *Handbook of Library Data Collection*[4] and the ALA committee charged with working with the International Standards Organization Z39 standards have used the concept. Regardless of one's position on the question, this may be the best tool to use when estimating the cost of being unable to efficiently return materials to the shelves. Take an average period of time in the library that will equal a week—be it five, six, or seven days—and count all reshelving activities during this period. This will result in raw data for a typical week's operation. Take the weekly reshelving figure and divide it by the number of books reshelved on average each hour. This yields the number of hours per week to reshelve materials. Multiply the hours figure by the hourly wage of the shelvers. This is your cost per week to shelve. If your shelves have exceeded working capacity, assume that shelvers are able to work at only 80% capacity. If this technique is used, the difference should be expressed in percentages: it costs X% more to shelve books in a crowded library.

Another technique to determine the cost of reshelving is to select a test area and actually time a shelver. Load a booktruck for an area that is not crowded and observe the time it takes for the truck to be shelved. This will provide an accurate estimate if the shelvers are unaware of the observation. When the shelvers are conscious of the fact that they are being timed, the Hawthorne Effect can take place.[5] If this happens, adjust the figures by 10 percent. Repeat the test using books from crowded shelving sections. The difference between the two tests represents the cost of crowded shelves to the library. In order to get a lump sum to use in the budget calculations, multiply this cost per item by the number circulated or the figure for the typical week. The typical week figure is then multiplied by 50 weeks. Use 50 weeks because there are generally ten days during a year when the operation is shut down due to holidays.

PERSONNEL

If a poor personnel situation is the reason for space reorganization, then the cost of not reorganizing will certainly be in the loss of productivity. Another cost of a personnel disturbance is the additional paper work generated: memos go back and forth; the procedures manual may have to be rewritten to provide documentation for some disciplinary activity. A strict division of labor—when one person refuses to do anything outside of clearly defined, specific tasks—costs the library in terms of productivity and resources required to deliver a service. The problem individual or individuals may also be producing work that must be redone or modified by others. A new procedure or check may be inserted into operations to side-step a recalcitrant employee. One way to calculate this cost is to use an operations research method: define a sample period and record the amount of time spent in activities caused by the problem staffer. Multiply that time by the hourly salary of the individuals involved, including the administrative staff.

Rarely is it possible to isolate an individual in a library work situation. When assessing the cost of a problem, therefore, look at all of the individuals affected and the amount of time lost by each. If the problem involves a specific service, then calculate the cost of that service. If it involves more than one area, consider costs for all of the areas involved.

REFERENCES

1. Philip D. Leighton and David C. Weber, *Planning Academic and Research Library Buildings*, 2nd Edition (Chicago: American Library Association, 1986): 51-5, 251-80.
2. Aaron Cohen and Elaine Cohen, *Automation, Space Management, and Productivity* (New York: R. R. Bowker, 1981): 100.
3. Robert Anthony, *Managment Accounting: Text and Cases*, 4th Edition (Homewood, Ill.: Richard D. Irwin, 1974) a good text with a useful chapter on cost determination.

   J. Lewis Brown and Leslie R. Howard, *Managerial Accounting and Finance* 4th Edition (Estover, Plymouth, U.K.: Macdonald & Evans, Ltd., 1982) contains a chapter on "Cost Benefit Analysis" that outlines the basic CBA procedure and also has a bibliography.

   E. J. Mishan, *Cost-Benefit Analysis: An informal introduction*, 4th Edition (London: Unwin Hyman, 1988) has "Some simplified examples of cost-benefit studies" as its first part, which some readers may find very useful.
4. Mary Jo Lynch, Editor, *Library Data Collection Handbook* (Chicago: American Library Association, Office for Research, 1981).
5. The Hawthorne Effect was so named as a result of experiments conducted in the 1930s at the Western Electric Company in Chicago. A series of five studies was conducted to determine the impact of changes in work environment on the productivity of assembly-line workers. One result that has remained in management literature is that workers were more productive when they were aware of the researchers and altered their productivity, regardless of the work environment. Since that time, the Hawthorne Effect has become a standard phrase to explain unusual increases in productivity when workers become aware that their output is being studied.

6 PUBLICITY

Publicity is an important component in the success of a library reorganization. A good publicity campaign pays dividends because the library's staff, administration, and clientele clearly understand the purposes and benefits of the reorganization. Wise use of publicity gains an understanding of and support for library operations after the project has been completed.

Plan a cohesive publicity campaign that can be carried out in staff time available. Each feature of the publicity should fit into the whole program; check the details of publicity planning before the first step of the move or reorganization is put into operation. Consultation with a publicity expert is also a good idea.

If the library staff does not include someone with public relations expertise, the project manager and library director should contact a community public relations expert—the editor of the local newspaper, a reporter from the television station, instructor from a local college or university—for tips and advice. Seeking outside advice further publicizes the up-coming project and builds community support. The outsider's viewpoint can prepare the staff for the public's reactions to the planned changes.

When a library staff, enlarged by helpers for a project, is participating in a move, there will always be extra tension and confusion. This atmosphere especially affects the abilities of the staff to perform regular library assignments—in addition to the assignments for the move. Communication helps alleviate the confusion and facilitates the smooth operation of the project.

Effective planning saves money and enables the publicity program to get off the ground. For example, if the library's copy equipment is out of service during the move, printing costs will increase the budget for publicity. The publicity plan may hinge on the use of special dittos or the library camera. Make sure all necessary equipment is rescued before the equipment is disconnected and packed. Locate live electrical outlets, an adequate number of extension cords, and a telephone line to remain live during the project, so that the personal computer and printer, electronic bulletin board, and other equipment necessary for producing the press releases, memoranda, etc. are running throughout the move.

All directions and directives must be easy to read and are most effective when accompanied by visuals. Pay attention to multilingual needs and make sure someone on the staff is familiar with all of the relevant languages. Consider the reading levels of the workers; some people are not functionally literate and most do not understand library jargon. Use simple, clear directions with plenty of arrows.

"Informal" publicity—casual conversations—are part of the

publicity process, just as they are part of any information-sharing process. Informal communication has its limitations, however. Publicity that has not been planned and organized may not reach the people who need to be contacted, and the message it carries may not be consistent. One of the major drawbacks of informal publicity is illustrated by the children's game "Telephone." One person whispers a sentence to another and the sentence is thus passed through a group. The last person announces what he or she has heard: the sentence is always far different from what it was at the beginning. As we all know, verbal messages get garbled in real life too, so take extra care to be clear and concise.

There is a need, however, to relay information in an informal manner because it is not feasible to write memos and press releases for everything. The space planner has to determine when to rely on informal conversations and when to structure the information disseminated about the move.

The amount of material needed for the publicity campaign depends on the particular situation and the individuals involved. Properly publicizing the move, both formally and informally, involves two categories of publicity: internal and external. Internal publicity is used with the library staff, contractors, and special workers hired for the move. External publicity is used to communicate with the community the library serves, the people using the facility during the period of disruption, and the governing body of the library.

INTERNAL PUBLICITY

Internal publicity is the best way to relay ideas and general instructions to all staff; it also creates a spirit of cooperation. The size of the staff, their ability to switch tasks and to work in particularly difficult situations, and the complexity of the space reorganization project determine the extent and degree of formality of the internal publicity effort. A staff of ten working in one room needs a minimal formal publicity program; a staff of 25 scattered in a number of branches requires an extensive campaign.

INFORMATION AND STYLE
The amount and type of information provided to staff will be a direct product of the management style in the library. A library

administration that does not routinely share information about decision making will have difficulty providing enough information to the staff about the reorganization. Conversely, the library administration that shares all information at all phases of operations with the staff will deluge the staff with details about the reorganization. Changing the management and communication style for the sake of a project is not always possible, or even desirable. The person in charge of the publicity will have to gear the amount of information to the prevailing management style in the library.

All organizations have a well-developed informal network, or "grapevine," which provides much of the information needed for daily operations. The space planner can use this grapevine to get accurate information to each of the nodes on the line, depending on the size of the reorganization.

As soon as the project manager is identified, she or he should evaluate the "information" on the informal network in light of the information which needs to be disseminated. The project manager must work closely with as many people as possible on the network to be sure the information circulated is accurate and helpful. There is really little to be done to refute rumors, but consider their existence and give them attention. This will be particularly important in regard to the budget and the amount of library funds budgeted for the move. Reorganization and retrenchment caused by fiscal problems mean an increased staff sensitivity to budget information. Other sensitive areas for rumor involve personnel changes as a result of the new space plan: who will be located where, changing reporting relationships, and how much individual work loads are going to change.

PRE-PROJECT STAFF PUBLICITY

Communicating with the staff should begin as soon as the decision is made to "do something." The library director should formally announce the project manager at a special staff meeting, or rely on a single written announcement. The entire staff should be aware of the reasons the shelves are being measured, the desks examined, and a consultant and the library space planner are asking them questions. Keeping all of the deliberations and investigations "a secret" while at the same time undertaking a detailed examination of facilities and operations delays implementation of the project and adversely affects morale.

Tools used for internal publicity are those already part of the everyday operation of the library. The existing house organ, such as the library newsletter, electronic bulletin board, or local network log-on message is a perfect place to begin. When the investigation is about to begin:

- include a paragraph outlining the problem
- devise a headline and/or logo for information about the project and use the same heading in every issue
- commit a regular section in the newsletter to the move or, if publication is infrequent, distribute memoranda and summary reports to *all* staff members.

Issue a special edition of the internal house organ if it is not scheduled to be published at the right time for the project. Use of the same format and color as the established house organ for the preliminary information demonstrates the project validity.

Another technique is to start a series of "project alerts." These are useful if the project information is too lengthy or complicated for inclusion in the regular newsletter or electronic bulletin board message, or if the staff must have daily information about the project's status. Follow the design and color of the regular library publication with perhaps one or two color reversals.

Timing is important in all project publicity, and it can be hampered by unavailable photocopiers, outlets, telephone lines, or supplies. Set up a copier with adequate supplies for occasions when information must be disseminated quickly. Send handwritten, photocopied memos if necessary—but get the information to the staff. Designate a temporary mailbox location for people whose work stations are in transit. Give top priority to distributing the notices in a timely fashion even if this means hand-delivering the news.

In addition to distributing copies, post all written communications in a conspicuous location. Consider preempting a traditional bulletin board for use during the operation. The best time to preempt a board is at the beginning of the project, when the information for the space data file is assembled. If there is no bulletin board, establish a space where notices will be posted.

Relay information to library staff before all of the decisions about the move are made. Library staff meetings are another vehicle for publicity. Carefully led discussion sessions encourage an open exchange of ideas. If the atmosphere in the library is such that there are rarely free and open discussions, divide the staff into smaller groups and ask each group to discuss one segment of the space reorganization and report back to the larger group. Each smaller group should have a recorder and a person responsible for representing the discussion to the space planner. If the meetings are held before the plan is finalized, the suggestions can be included in the plan.

Notes and status reports added to the daily log-on message of the library's online system are an excellent way to keep staff up to date. Establish a special file in the system—"Move Status"— which contains important information. If the CRT's are tied up as part of the move, put the information on a file in a microcomputer staff will be able to access. Relay move information also via closed-circuit video screens or the local access cable TV channel. If a video system is in the library, use it; if it is part of the college or school or local cable bulletin board, submit information to be included in daily announcements. The information published in the special issues of the newsletter or special daily memos may be duplicated. The information should be repeated in several locations in case someone misses the posted notices.

New approaches to jobs will develop as the implementation of the space plan moves forward and materials and offices are relocated. People cannot be forced to read all of the information available, but the information should be accessible. Don't try to save money by skimping on information or forcing staff to take extra steps to get to it. Maximum dissemination of publicity is important for the operation; it will establish a cooperative atmosphere.

ASSESSING INFORMATION REQUIREMENTS

Staff members have different needs, not only in relation to their planned roles in the project, but also in relation to their need to know about operations in order to do a job. Individuals who serve at the public information desk need enough information to give patrons correct responses. A librarian sitting next to a sign that says "information" looks silly when he or she cannot respond adequately to a patron's questions about why books are stacked in boxes. The staff member should be knowledgeable enough to answer that the library is moving materials to better serve the patrons because of overcrowded shelves.

Whatever reason is given, unsolicited advice from patrons is guaranteed. A properly informed staff member will be able to respond to this "advice" in a way that will help the library. The decision to continue operations and the extent of the operations during a move will define the scope and amount of information needed for the patrons.

Staff involved with the preliminary measurements and inventories should be aware of the reasons for their activities. The chances of obtaining accurate measurements are increased if the importance of the task and its role in the resolution of a library problem is explained. When giving instructions for the measuring process at a group meeting, allocate time to present an overview of the problem and the planning program and request immediate feedback; this helps people retain a sense of their value to the success of the project.

As the tasks are assigned, relay the information to individuals verbally, but keep written instructions; they help supervisors keep the project moving and form a part of the publicity picture. The instructions will have to cover possible problems and details of each task. The text of the publicity can be drawn from these instructions.

The pattern for staff information during all phases of the project is set at the inventory stage. A summarizing cover memo attached to the instructions for inventory teams will put the inventory process in context, and the staff will be able to appreciate the complexity of the overall project.

DURING THE MOVE

The project manager has the task of keeping everyone informed of each element in the timing chain and may have to delegate other reponsibilities of the project in the interest of good communications. It may be useful to appoint someone as the "communicator," or the contact person, to help the timing of each of the teams during the move.

When a move is in progress, so much is going on that there is a tendency to forget about communication and publicity for the staff and to concentrate on keeping the users and the parent organization informed. This can delay the move, cause errors, and slow the postmove adjustments. One library was in the middle of moving to a new building; when halfway through, a volunteer approached a supervisor and pointed out that for some time the shelves "hadn't looked quite right." It turned out that the shelves had been installed incorrectly and a major realignment was required. Because the worker hesitated to communicate this concern immediately, the project was delayed. An open exchange of information when the work was underway might have uncovered the problem sooner.

To get all of the feedback needed, encourage workers to record observations as they occur by using a suggestion box, tape recorder, or laptop computer. Library staff members should be encouraged to chat informally with the movers, especially about the progress and problems of the move, as long as the informal conversation does not impede the progress of the move. Take notes at the regular staff meetings held during the move. Those notes provide a record for the final report and inform the absent staff members of progress. When several groups are meeting during one day, take notes at each meeting so a record is made of the agreements reached by each group.

Daily notices in the special move newsletter or in the regular library newsletter are important. Praise those workers who are doing their jobs well in a section of the daily notices. Use personalized tools; perhaps a "worker of the week" or a "quote of the day" can be included in the release. Set a schedule for the information to be released—daily, every two days, at noon, and at closing— whatever seems to be the most effective for the staff and the magnitude of the project. Then inform everyone involved of the schedule and meet it.

Even if the status of the move has not changed, the release should go out on schedule as promised. If there is no change in the message, keep it, but change the date. Or use visuals. For instance, it may take several days to construct shelves. The daily notice can identify the number of shleves to go up and consist of a simplified layout that shows each day's accomplishments. A spreadsheet program such as Lotus 1-2-3 will easily convert the progress to a pie chart which can be printed and posted. If the current task involves shifting books, an acetate layout may be used and marked as each section is shifted or show circulation or catalog terminals as they are brought online.

Outside factors can delay operations. For instance, rain will postpone shifting books from one building to another if the booktrucks are uncovered; shelving may not be delivered on time; elevators can break down and defy repair for days on end; new equipment arrives without needed parts. Reasons for the delay should be printed in the news bulletin, especially as they affect daily goals.

Throughout the move, remember the need to release information after project completion, and gather the relevant information during the move for the post-move publicity. The post-move party for volunteers will be made more interesting by displaying photographs of various project phases.

AFTER THE MOVE

The project is a cohesive operation. Publicity during one phase leads logically to the next. Using the same publicity techniques in the post-move operations as used in the pre-move operations maintains continuity. In addition, communications channels established during the move may be useful for library operations after the space project ends. Project publicity techniques may help establish a viable channel for the regular dissemination of library information.

Internal publicity after the move provides information about the new locations of materials, equipment, service points, and staff members. If one unit or department has been moved or rearranged, all of the departments have to be aware of this. Accompany announcements of the rearrangements with explanations, even if these are only a rough diagram of the new collection arrangement, equipment arrangment, or revised work flow.

Make staff aware of the new locations for materials if all or even part of the collection has been moved. Schedule brief sessions to review the revised layout. Also review the collection arrangment if it has changed. If part of the classification schedule has been moved to another location and the collection sequence no longer runs consecutively from A to Z or 000 to 999, the staff has to know.

Give equal consideration to publicizing the revised work patterns, which are inevitable because desks, offices, or computer terminals were moved. The staff bulletin board may have been moved and a new location established for sending or receiving notices and mail. Publicity for staff about new locations of files and people will expedite the formal adoption of the space arrangement and perhaps expedite the informal arrangements. A project to absorb one library into another will be incomplete and confusion will reign unless there are new maps of offices, files, and the collection. An orientation tour is desirable. Withhold permanent revisions in expensive publications until time has elapsed for the new arrangment to settle. Delay making permanent range-finders until the collection has been used for at least a week.

EXTERNAL PUBLICITY

A good publicity program is the key to avoiding unnecessary patron confusion and repetitious explanations. The primary purpose of publicity is to educate the users and the library community about the changes taking place in the library. When the move is in progress, the intent is to inform the patrons of any service changes and the extent of the interim operations. After the move, the publicity informs the users and library community of the library's new status.

Whatever the reason for the move, the publicity should be

worded so the users and the community can understand the rationale. For example, publicity about a space reorganization making way for a new service should include information about the new service in each release. Learn from commercial enterprises that have the ubiquitous sign posted, "Reopening soon to serve you better," or "Pardon our confusion/mess/dust/... we are remodeling to serve you better." After all, the primary objective of moves and projects is to make it possible for the library to serve its patrons better.

Use the library's logo (or have one designed for the move) on a all relases. The logo helps the notices stand out and immediately identifies the source for the reader. Use the public relations capabilities of the library staff to the fullest. Ask the writers to write, the speakers to speak, and the artists to draw, to generate eye-catching, informative copy. Information about the project should be the priority in the library's public relations program. Astute library administrators have used a move to another location as a springboard for disseminating information about the library and its functions.

WHAT INFORMATION?

The press release is a popular communication channel.[1] Press release format is recommended for writing any short information release, particularly for external users. Components of an effective press release include:

Dates: Include the dates of the move and the date of the release.

Objective of the project: State this briefly and do not use library jargon.

Services available: If the reference desk will be closed, say so; if services will continue uninterrupted, say so.

Special services during the move: Will someone page materials?

Change of hours: If the hours will change, list new hours; if they don't, list regular hours of operation because someone will remember his or her overdue book or vidoetape only after reading the press release.

Duration of the project: If a completion date is set, include this information, or indicate the length of time the project is to take and a possible starting date. Do not make a promise which cannot be kept. If there is uncertainty about the availability of helpers or equipment or wiring, extend the announced completion date.

Special contact person: Include the name, address, and phone number of the person who can be contacted for more information about the contents of the release.

Issue the first press release with pre-move announcements. Then revise the release during the move with updated information about curtailed library hours or activities. If the move is scheduled to take place over an extended period of time, issue a release at regular intervals during the process to keep the changes in the minds of the patrons and the library community.

PUBLICITY CHANNELS

Publicity about the move should be released widely. Consider several campaigns aimed at different target groups. Each communication channel will require a slightly different form of information packaging.

Of the many possible places for getting the message out, local newspapers and news media are at the top of the list. The local daily newspaper will usually print well-worded releases when it has room. Check the editorial policy before flooding the offices with information. The chances of a story or release getting into print are greater if pictures accompany the story. Remember, though, that the use of photographs and news releases is at the discretion of the news editor, and so the person preparing the releases should try to follow local policies. When the planner convinces a newspaper to run progress reports during the move, there will be a line limit, as well as guidelines for the information the paper would prefer. Find out what format and style are required because move information can become garbled if edited improperly.

Send news releases to the local commercial television channels and radio stations as well. Local cable television stations carrying public-access channels may agree to air one screen of information or at least a five-second spot for free. Take advantage of this, and send information such as "10,000 books are to be moved to Smith School on August 14. The task will take an estimated 1,000 people-hours. Potential volunteers please call 123-4567 for more information." Include the press release information on the log-on screen or public message section of dial-access catalogs.

Include a few sentences about the library move in the daily announcements to the staff and students in the school system. The public library which is heavily used by students at a neighboring school or college should request the addition of a few sentences of information to the regular announcements used in these institutions. Teachers and students whose assignment deadlines are based on library access will appreciate the notification.

Publicity for the special library within an organization should include at least one memo to all department heads and notices posted on staff bulletin boards as well as the electronic mail system. Use the union newsletters, want ad digests, and announcements in the cafeteria to get information to company personnel. Each information release should include a sentence as to the availability of materials and staff.

A public library can send notices to the local service clubs for announcement at regular meetings. Not only are these clubs a good source of volunteers, but the members often constitute a cross-section of the community and will help the information reach a large number of people. The library space planner could also be a featured speaker at these meetings.

A mailing to a special segment of the library's clientele is a channel for information which can be used in any type of library. A very small library with up-to-date borrower records is a good candidate for this type of mailing. Include a clear statement of how the change will affect the identified clientele, addressing all anticipated concerns. Name one individual whom patrons may contact by telephone or at the information desk for the duration of the move. This person should have a detailed grasp of the move and be able to help, or to tactfully explain why he or she cannot offer assistance at that time. In a larger library, identify users of a particular service and send them a flyer—for example, the users of the patent service or the regular users of the database search services.

Replace the usual prerecorded message about library hours and activities on one of the "general information" phone lines with one giving information on the move and its effects on services. Record the message for playback before the caller is connected to a staff member. Since several styles of answering machines are available, check with local suppliers of business equipment to find one that can handle the call load. Home answering machines are designed for a far different call load than the answering machines used by a movie theater, for example.

Because a reorganization will always inconvenience someone, a library staff member should be assigned the task of listening to the complaints and providing emergency assistance when appropriate. A project in an academic library will be inconvenient regardless of attempts to schedule the activity during a slow period in an academic cycle. When the copying machine is out of service, you can be sure that at least one career will depend on getting a grant request copied; a student about to finish a paper will need to recheck one citation; and an important speech can be completed only after a librarian looks up the Latin idiom. In many libraries the regular patrons will believe that the "closed" sign refers to everyone else. This is a particular problem in a law library or special library. An ombudsman can see that many of these tasks are performed or can locate alternate sources to meet patron requirements. If the staff is not large enough to designate an ombudsman, look for a volunteer capable of doing the job.

PICTURES

Pictures are important, particularly for the mid-move publicity release. The school photography class or the community photography club will be able to suggest names of photographers if an in-house photographer is not available. If the parent organization has a public relations department, its photographer might be availabe for extra assignments.

For press releases use black-and-white photographs only. Make several prints of the appropriate photo and include one with all news announcements sent out. The pictures may or may not be used, but without them, the story loses an extra dimension. Do not expect the return of photographs sent to publicity channels.

Pictures are also important for library records. Both color and black-and-white photos taken before, during, and after the move provide historic illustrations. Communications and presentations following the move will be more lively when enhanced by a slide-tape program. When funds or personnel for the project have been provided by an outside organization or an individual, express appreciation by framing and inscribing a photograph of the library in its new configuration.

Work closely with the photographer to get the best pictures. Staff pictures and picture-taking sessions help raise morale; make sure that every individual involved in the operation is clear in at least one on-the-job photo. Where many volunteers are used, the library should make a visual presentation to the agencies that have provided the help. Pictures of the move are also useful in illustrated annual reports. Videotape key segments of the library before the move begins and in their new status after the move ends. Include "action shots" of various people working on the project. Show the videotape continuously during the post move celebration.

CELEBRATION

Arrange a party to recognize the work of the volunteers. After-the-fact "thank you" press releases should include black-and-white photographs taken during the party. The videotape can be shown on the institution's video "bulletin board," where it will encourage conversation and help to get the message across to the patrons throughout the move and after the party. If it is the right size, it may be possible to have the tape aired on the local-access channel of cable television. Consider giving the volunteers a "thank you" video tape showing "before" and "after" shots of the building as well as shots of each volunteer. A celebration event prolongs confusion but provides that valuable additional time for the staff to adjust to the new surroundings before tackling the backlogs of work.

The post-move publicity for patrons will follow the pattern for publicity normally used by the library. Introduce the new library configuration using an "inauguration"; in the case of a remodeled building, a reception or formal dedication is appropriate. Invited guests should include members of the construction staff, dignitaries, and the individuals responsible for the renovation and move. The degree of formality of the occasion is a judgment made by the library administration or the parent organization.

Consider purchasing mementos of the occasion as gifts for the workers. Tee shirts are popular, albeit expensive. Buttons and badges are always appreciated and maximize publicity for the activity. Commission a commemorative poster as a gift item.

An internally produced brochure containing reproductions of business cards combined with "thank you" will express appreciation to the store that contributed the boxes, the business that gave the punch, the people who baked cookies, the fire department or police force that provided extra security, and those businesses and individuals who helped with the move but who are unable to attend the celebration.

Publicity for the new library configuration provides a good opportunity to introduce a new logo, organizational structure, or service, or to focus attention on a special feature of the library. A good publicity program will facilitate major changes in library operations and accent the ongoing operations of the library. Take a lead from all of the commercial products and announce the "new improved" library; it certainly will be.

REFERENCES

1. Mona Garvey, *Library Public Relations: A Practical Handbook* (New York: H.W. Wilson, 1980) Chap. 7, and Anne F. Roberts and Susan Griswold Blandy, *Public Relations for Librarians* (Englewood, Colo.: Libraries Unlimited, 1989) are both good sources for information on constructing press releases and dealing with the news media. Another excellent work on public relations is K.C. Harrison, *Public Relations for Public Librarians*, 2nd Edition, rev. (Hampshire, England: Gower Publishing Company, 1982).

7 STARTING THE PROJECT

Once the goals of the project have been defined; data have been gathered about the collection, furnishings, and equipment; and an alternative arrangement to address the space problem has been chosen for implementation, detailed plans for putting the new space plan into place must be drawn up. Before the project can begin, layouts must be completed, the move method selected, timetables set, the work force selected, and plans made for continuing library operations for the project's duration.

LAYOUTS

Before personnel are hired, or timetables set, or the move method selected, complete and detailed layouts must be drawn. Layouts help in the decision making process by showing what furniture and equipment will fit where, even if temporarily. Final layouts show exactly where items and collections will be located at the end of the project. The layouts are especially critical if a professional moving company is hired or if the project manager plans to have many subprojects in action simultaneously.

The space data files, which include floor plans produced during the assessment and measuring processes, are used to draw the layouts. The dimension information gathered can be visually represented by cutting to scale pieces of cardboard to represent furniture and equipment and indicating the name of each item. When the pieces are placed on an accurate floor plan, the overall effect of the arrangement will be evident. The same can be done for the collections, using miniature representations of the shelving sections marked with the correct call-number allocations.

CAD (Computer Assisted Design) programs are valuable helps in layout preparation. Before the project reaches this stage, the program should be installed and the library space planner should be familiar with its operation. Adequate RAM and a mouse are important requirement for CAD programs. Since learning a CAD program takes time, be sure to block out enough time to learn how to use it.

The number of layouts to be drawn is a function of the complexity of the move. In a small, one-floor library, it is possible to have all of the collections and furnishing on one layout. For complex moves, though, a series of layouts for each floor may be necessary. Separate layouts will show telecommunications lines and electrical wiring, with line changes and instruments marked in the appropriate location; the furniture locations; plumbing; and interior finishes such as painting. The collection layout can be as detailed as the library needs. It must be accurate and clearly marked so the supervisors and those responsible for the move can understand where each part and section of the collection should be located. Markings should include call-number allocations for sections. A separate layout of office or work space will be required if professional movers are used.

If an architect has been hired to work on a renovation or addition, he or she will provide layouts. These, however, usually only mark in the shelving or note the parameters of the ranges. Assigning the collection to an area is the respsonsibility of the space planner. Use the architect's layout as the basic drawing and add collection and furnishings layout information. If the architect's contract calls for interior design, furnishings will be included.

Matching existing furniture to space is a detailed, time consuming process which can be expedited during the layout process. Make sure the furniture drawn on the layout has the same dimensions as the existing furnishings if they are to be re-used in the new configuration. Furnishing plans may have to be altered, particularly if there have been significant cost over-runs during construction.

TIMETABLES

How does the library space planner set up a project timetable? Many planners and/or administrators automatically estimate time lines without dividing the process into formal steps. However, tools are available for planning the sequence of events and estimating the time needed to complete the total project, as well as individual segments. The methods offer formal structure and identify the most cost-efficient choices for getting the job done. Once the sequence of events is devised, the time-frame estimates and timetables can be developed methodically to the level of sophistication and complexity most appropriate for the project.

The Performance Evaluation Review Technique or PERT chart is a popular planning tool for ordering and organizing a project. If used to its fullest capacity, it requires a team of people to design it and intepret it; modified versions of the PERT Chart force the planner and supevisor to see what steps must be completed before

FIGURE 1

PERT Chart for access services.

Access Services: Sequence of Events for Moving Microforms, Reserve, and Archives

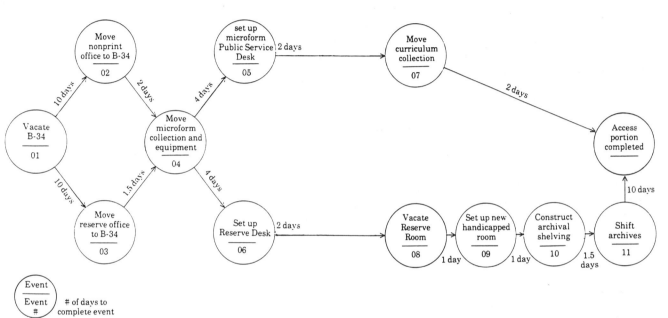

the next step can begin and illustrates which actions can be carried out concurrently.

Figure 1 is an example of a PERT Chart used to create a move timetable for microforms, reserve, and archives. Each event or action on the chart tells the manager two things: the order of the event in the overall move and the time necessary to complete the event. The planner determines the estimated time for the entire project by totaling the listed time segments.

Once completed, the chart graphically illustrates the sequence of activities. Copies of the chart are useful to the staff participating in the move and also for disseminating information to the public.

The Gantt Chart is another tool used to plan project sequence and timing. It too illustrates concurrent steps in the overall project and provides a graphic indication of start and end dates. In Figure 2 the Gantt chart is used to create a timetable for a complex move. Many steps were needed to reach the objective of the move: centralization of reference from divisional subject areas. Gantt charts are constructed by listing events in the left column; time divisions are placed along the top. The latter are listed as weeks, months, days, hours, or other segments useful to the project

Figure 2. GANTT Chart for planning the centralization of Reference.

```
------------------------------------------------------------------------------------------------
                                            D A Y   D A Y   D A Y   D A Y   D A Y   D A Y   D A Y   D A Y   D A Y   D A Y
                            TASK             1     2     3     4     5     6     7     8     9    10    11    12    13    14    15    16    17    18    19   20

Construct warehouse shelving in storage area  XXXXXXXXXXXX
Move archival coll. into new storage area             XXXXXXXXXXXXXXXXXX
Clean and rehang vacated shelving                     XXXXXXXXXXXXXX
Move Dewey collection into vacated shelving                  XXXXXXXXXXXXXXXX
Clean and rehang shelving vacated by Dewey                     XXXXXXXXXXXXXXXX
Construct shelving for LC collection                           XXXXXXXXXXX
Shift LC collection onto newly constructed shelving                 XXXXXXXXXXXXXXXX
Construct display shelving                                   XXXXXXXXX
Move periodicals collection into vacated Dewey shelving           XXXXXXXXXXXXXXXXXXXXXXXXXXXXX
Move periodicals display                                             XXXX
Move periodicals' offices and workstations                                XXXX
Move microforms into new periodicals area                                      XXXXXXXX
Realign, construct shelving in former periodicals area                         XXXXXXXXXXXX
Move reference coll. into former periodicals area                                  XXXXXXXXXXXX
Move reference offices                                                             XXXXXXXXXXXX
```

Figure 3. GANTT Chart for Time/Motion study.

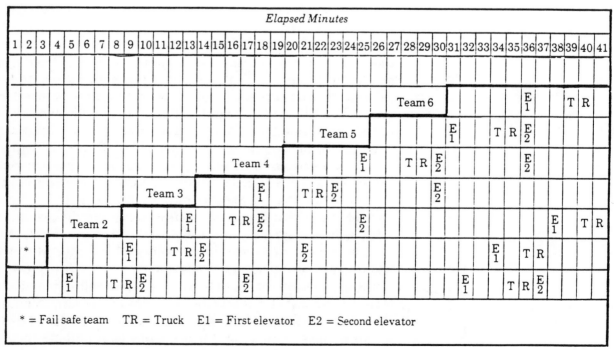

planner. Gantt charts work well for planning project timetables where the events are separate, sequential, and dependent.

Figure 3 is another Gantt Chart created to time moving teams that had two elevators to transport an entire collection between two buildings. Pre-move time and motion studies provided raw data for estimating how long each component of the project would take. Figure 3 plans how six teams (plus one "fail-safe team") will move from an old building to a new building, with only one small elevator at each site. This illustration shows how long it should take to transport a loaded booktruck to the new site and return an empty truck for reloading. In the illustration, Team 1 leaves first; the "fail-safe" team departs six minutes later; Team 2 departs 16 minutes later; Team 3 departs 26 minutes later, etc. Using the time it takes to complete a run as a base figure, it is possible to determine the number of teams and trucks needed to keep the move flowing smoothly.

OPERATIONS RESEARCH TECHNIQUES

Operations research tests involve moving a small segment of the collection through the project steps along the anticipated routes of travel. Figure 4 illustrates an operations research timing test using wooden troughs. This type of test can serve as an inexpensive way to determine how each section of a collection should be packed and transported. Results will yield information about the amount of time it will take to pack and walk each section of the collection to the new location. It clarifies the most efficient order for unpacking and setting up at the new location and the best form of team grouping. Records should be kept of the amount time expended on each task and the impact of the different traffic patterns on the total time involved in completing the task.

When performing an operations research test, teams are used to do a trial walk-through of the move. The size of the team is determined by the task to be completed. Make a trial run with a team of two people, then assign a team of three people to to the same task and repeat the run. Three is a common number of team members for packing materials: one person takes the books off the shelf; another loads them onto the booktruck or packs them into cartons; and a third labels the truck or carton, makes certain that

FIGURE 4. OPERATIONS RESEARCH TIME STUDY: TIMING OF MOVE USING TROUGHS

We have just completed a trial "timing run." The following times are the averages recorded using one hand-truck with four troughs, containing a total of 100 volumes.

Loading books into holders, labeling and placing on dollies	4 min. 57 sec.
Moving truck to freight elevator	1 min. 25 sec.
Old basement to new basement (wheeling dollies)	6 min. 35 sec.
Basement to shelf	2 min. 30 sec.
Unload books	10 min. 53 sec.
TOTAL TO GET BOOKS TO BUILDING	26 min. 20 sec.
Time to return empty dollie and troughs to old building entrance	4 min. 26 sec.
Return to Library using back elevator	3 min. 33 sec.
GRAND TOTAL: TIME TO BRING 100 VOLUMES TO NEW LIBRARY AND RETURN CONTAINERS FOR REFILL	34 min. 19 sec.

Trial runs were also conducted using a booktruck. Total time from basement to basement with full book trucks was 6 minutes, 30 seconds. The men had to complete two extra lifting motions loading the truck, and unloading at a higher level when we reached the loading dock.

There were no ramps to load and unload the dollies onto the truck which could have saved time. In addition, the platform for the loading dock is too high, an additional ramp would have to be constructed here.

THESE FIGURES WERE COMPILED WHEN MEN WERE "FRESH" AND BEGINNING THE JOB; NO OTHER FACTORS ARE CALCULATED INTO THE FIGURES.

materials are going into the truck in the proper order, and moves the trucks or boxes to a holding area for the next team to take over. A two-person team can also be used. One person takes the material from the shelf and puts it in the packing container; the other person checks the contents for order, then closes and labels the container.

If the move route leads to a point outside the library, a second team takes the full booktrucks from the holding area to the point at which the materials leave the building. If there is an obstacle such as an elevator, a ramp, or an extra-long hallway to cross, then a third team has the sole responsibility of making sure the materials, whether loaded trucks or boxes on flatbed trucks, successfully traverse the obstacle. At the point where the materials enter the other building, a fourth team is needed to make certain the entry is smooth and the materials get to the correct point in the new stacks. When the materials arrive at the stacks, a fifth team unloads the books from the containers and shelves the material. At least one person at the final site is responsible for making sure the materials are put on the correct shelves in order.

PEOPLE HOURS

The best way to define the amount of help needed is by counting people hours. If the study showed it would take a person on Team One .5 hours to unload a range, and Team One has three people, then 1.5 hours per range are required to unload shelves. If Team Two has two members and it takes them one hour to move the loaded boxes or shelves to another area, then a total of two hours of help are needed to complete that segment of the move for that range.

The amount of staff needed is determined by calculating the people-hours required for each phase of the operation and adding them together for the total number of hours needed. Add 15 percent to the total for slippage, since unforseen delays and turnover will affect work hours: the elevators break down, part of the crew is allergic to the dust, construction is delayed or even incomplete. Absenteeism also reduces the size of the workforce. If the actual workforce is smaller than indicated in the test phase, it will take longer to do the job.

Contingency plans are needed to insure that the entire workforce is busy throughout the project. The space planner working with several unions and volunteers from different organizations, work release prisoners, the vagaries of academic schedules, or the ebb and flow of a seasonal business has to consider the impact of external forces on the schedule and ability to complete the tasks. The productivity of workers during the move will vary. Workers start slowly as they learn the task. Then there is a brief flurry of activity as they discover they are able to do the work very quickly. The next adjustment will be to a relatively steady pace for a brief period, followed by a slow-down as the relative monotony of the work sets in. If 400 hours of help are needed, plan to acquire at least 460 hours.

Consult Figure 5, Practical Variations, for a comparison of move methods, time required to complete projects, number of

Figure 5. Practical variations.*

No. vols.	Staff	Time	Method	New/Same Building	Type of Library
182 Bays; Archives	Maintenance	6 wks.	Boxes	N	Archive
7,000+; 80 periodicals	3 (2 students)	48 hrs.	Garbage bags	N	School
12,000	Students	1 day	Hand carry	S	School
12,000	Volunteers	3 hrs.	Hand carry	N	Public
15,000	Staff	1 day	Book-truck	N	Public
21,000	Students	4 hrs.	Boxes	N	Academic
22,000	40 (including volunteers	1 day	Boxes	N	Academic
26,000	Students	5 wks.	Pine boxes	N	Academic
35,000	Volunteers	1 day	Hand carry	S	Academic
45,000	50 Volunteers	2 days	Boxes	N	Public
60,000	Temp help	8 days	Book-truck	N	Academic
95,000	Prof. mover, janitors	17.5 days	Boxes and hand-pass	N	Law/Special
100,000	Students/ volunteers	1 day	NA	N	Law/ University
320,000	Staff/ students	25 days	NA	N	Law
360,000	Prof. movers	NA	Boxes	N	Public
400,000	Prof. movers (nights)	100 hrs.	Boxes	N	Public
450,000	Staff/ students	NA	Special trucks	N	Academic

470,000	Students	6 wks.	Pine boxes	S	Academic
600,000	Prof. movers	NA	Beer cartons	N	Public
700,000	Prof. movers	200 hrs.	Special carts	N	Academic
850,000	Students	59 days	Special book-truck	N	Academic
1,000,000	Students/ mainten- ance	60 days	Boxes	N	Special
2,000,000	Prof. movers	2 yrs.	Closed boxes	N	Public

*This information was drawn from reports of library moves in the literature.

staff, and number of volumes in a variety of moves reported in library literature. This shows there is no standard number of items that can be moved, no matter which method for moving is used. Figure 5 may provide some additional guidance to the planner who is desgning a timetable and trying to estimate personnel needs.

SELECTING THE METHOD

A number of methods are used to move library collections, ranging from hand-passing material, charging out all material; using booktrucks, boxes, and specially constructed troughs. When the collection is going into empty space, a move is fairly straightforward. But if an overcrowded collection is rearranged or a new shelving procedure is introduced, a step is added as backshifting, stacking, or temporarily storing materials is needed.

Combining several move methods may work best. For example, a move to a new public library used a book brigade to pick up numbered sacks of books. Elementary school children assisted in the move by picking up the sacks, boarding a school bus for a ride to the new building, and handing the sacks over to volunteers waiting in the new library.

BOOKTRUCKS

Booktrucks are one of the most popular ways of moving collections. As the trucks are easily moved on to elevators and across floors, they eliminate a lot of the heavy lifting involved in other methods. Do not underestimate the wear and tear on booktrucks used for a move.

Examine the book trucks to be used in the move, as well as the move route. In one move of a branch collection of a research library, the main library's booktrucks were wheeled across the campus to the branch to ensure that enough trucks were on-site at the branch. The booktrucks were inexpensive, as became obvious when many "died" after the cross-campus trek to and from the branch. The wheel shafts of the trucks were not reinforced, and they were bent beyond repair.

One of the disadvantages of using booktrucks is their cost. If the path of the move is uneven and the booktrucks are aging or of poor quality, using them for a move may speed their destruction and require expensive equipment replacement. Trucks cost a minimum of $150 each; it is an expensive proposition to purchase enough trucks to keep a steady chain moving from location to location. Booktrucks with flat shelves are not good for moving collections since books will fall through on to the floor when the trucks are moving. If the library has many flatbed booktrucks and plans to move the collection using them, then either purchase more trucks or use the flatbed trucks to transport boxes full of books.

BOXES

Another favorite method for moving collections is boxing the materials. This tried-and-true method is a carry-over from college days when liquor and grocery store boxes were used to move possessions from dormitory to home to apartment. Generally, the boxes from liquor stores are preferable; they are stronger and less likely to contain bugs or dirt than grocery boxes. When liquor store boxes are available, check to see if they will hold books. This means they must be sturdy, clean, and have lids. Boxes of varying sizes should not be used since they do not stack evenly. Lids or covers are necessary to protect the contents from rain and snow and to make stacking easier.

Boxes purchased especially for moving are ideal. They are available in either 30″ or 36″ square sizes and are quickly assembled with tape. Professional movers use these boxes and construct them onsite using pre-glued reinforced tape. Movers' boxes are best because they are sturdy and clean, are put together quickly,

BUILDING BOOK TROUGHS

Although one method for trough construction has them built the same length as the average shelf, 36″ long, we suggest troughs be built 30″ long because the 36″ trough, when loaded, can weigh over 50 pounds, making it difficult to lift. When the trough's angle and the slant are correct, it can be filled, carried, and lined up on a freight truck with little problem. The planners from one library found a few hospital stretchers in storage and used them to provide a support frame for the carefully numbered troughs lined up end to end. The stretcher was filled with troughs and one team was able to move all of the books from a single-faced three-foot section of shelves. The stretcher was lined up outside the ranges and the troughs brought into the stacks on a flatbed booktruck, thus avoiding the problem of stacking troughs out of order.

can be sealed, and, because they are all the same size, can be stacked.

Ideally, one box will hold one shelf of books from a circulating collection. If the shelves are to be refilled two-thirds full—the acceptable definition of "working capacity"—then purchase a 30″ box and allow for one shelf of books per box. When filling premarked boxes to the "working capacity" measurement, allow more boxes for oversized books and special-collection materials. The weight of law books significantly reduces the life of a moving box.

Non-library packers will be inclined to fill a box, as opposed to loading a set number of volumes from a shelf. Although this increases the number of books moved, it results in boxes that are heavier, making them more difficult to lift and to move, and slows the unpacking process because of the inevitable loss of sequence.

Boxes wear out and are damaged when they are loaded into trucks and other moving equipment. Ordering a box for every shelf of books is not necessary if boxes are unpacked immediately and turned around for reloading. A rough guide is to plan for four to five trips per box. Order extras to be kept at the reshelving points in case of damage—and order extra box tape because some repairs will be necessary before boxes are reused. If planning to store the collection in the boxes, order enough boxes for each shelf of books.

BOOK-TROUGHS

Another moving device is the custom-made carrier or book trough. Book troughs are economical and are the most desirable alternative in a situation where there are not enough new sturdy booktrucks to handle a move and monies are not available for purchasing more. If the plant department or custodial staff do carpentry work, the trough might be the best option.

The advantage of the trough is that it is easily constructed and can be used over and over during the course of the move. After the move, it is a nice bookshelf that fits on a desk.

HANDPASSING

Handpassing books along a "chain" of people is another moving method. It is most ideal for relatively small moves of book collections, where large numbers of volunteers can be recruited to work for no more than two hours each. This method also works well if elevators are not in the move path and books need to get up the stairs, around corners, and into areas difficult to access with booktrucks or dollies. Handpassing is best used for collections of fiction or children's works. Science and law books are heavier and more likely to be dropped, slowing the chain and damaging the books.

At the start and end points, supervisors should make sure books are removed from the shelves in order and are reshelved in order. At least one roving supervisor is needed to keep the line flowing smoothly and to watch for people who are becoming bored or fatigued so they can be moved to another task. Fatigued people will start dropping books, damaging the items and slowing the overall effort. The spacing on the chain depends on the age and reach of the volunteers. People on the chain should be able to pass books to each other without much movement. Starts and stops of materials will have to be coordinated and the collection layout followed closely at the receiving end.

INTERNAL SHIFTS

One of the most important—and most frequently overlooked—aspects of the internal space-reallocation process is realizing ahead of time that there must be an empty section in order to start the move. The next problem is to select the most efficient space to be empty. The empty space should be at least one section of empty shelves or, most likely, a number of ranges. The empty section should be at the beginning point of the new collection arrangement. The starting point should be marked on the layout.

If shelving cannot be freed, consider using available floor space. If enough space out of the mainstream of traffic is cleared, books can be stacked on the floors. Stacking on the floor is fine as long as the boxes and materials to be shelved first are easily accessed. Booktrucks are another alternative for storing books temporarily. At the beginning of the process, make sure that the library has enough trucks to hold the stored books and to carry out other functions.

"Walk through" the entire shift to assure a continuing supply of appropriate empty shelves. New collection arrangements and sequences may generate logjams if empty space midpoint in the shift is not available.

The real talent in internal shifting lies in the ability to make sure that, at the end of the shift, the empty shelves will be those destined to house the materials temporarily stored in the boxes, on the floors, or on the booktrucks.

BACKSHIFTS

Backshifts are often the most reasonable way to implement an internal move; the decision to use this technique must be made early in the project. An advantage of backshifting over storing the materials on the floor, on trucks, or in boxes is the retention of the call-number sequence; this saves time and effort.

When there is not enough extra shelving to construct new ranges to hold the materials, or there is not enough floor space or booktrucks to stack the number of volumes being temporarily dislocated, then the alternative is to backshift. Backshift is accomplished by crowding books into the existing shelving while retaining the call number sequence. Use the tops, bases, and full shelves in order to get empty sections to start the move. Overcrowding existing shelves generates empty space.

Layouts are the key to planning the backshift, since they allow the planner to move imaginary sections of materials before actually sifting the items. When occupied shelving is to be disassembled and reused, backshifting allows the planner to remove the books on those shelves to a "holding" area while the shelves are disassembled and then reassembled. If the operation is a large one and big sections of materials are to be relocated, at least one layout is needed to make certain that the books will have a temporary location during the tear-down and reconstruction of shelving. Since books are handled twice, the project manager will have to monitor each shift closely to keep things in order.

THE WORKFORCE

The workforce for the move may include professional movers, contractors, students, volunteers, library staff, and temporary help. The type of workforce not only depends upon availability, but upon the budget, level and difficulty of the move, the sheer magnitude of the move, and workforce pool.

LIBRARY STAFF

Union contracts, civil service regulations, or institutional regulations may govern the work assignments of full-time staff members. Understand these regulations thoroughly before making staff utilization plans and pay particular attention to job descriptions and work hours.

The skills needed to move materials are different from those needed in normal library operations. Ask for volunteers from the staff and check the library personnel folders to see who has relevant experience or skills for the move. Of course, the same person cannot be expected to carry out his or her regular job duties and fulfill extra duties for a move; regular operations will have to be temporarily modified or extra staff hired for move-related activities.

When the library is to be moved after regular operating hours, the library staff should be given the option of working overtime. This expedites the activity, reduces worker-training time, and provides an opportunity for the staff to earn extra money.

TEMPORARY WORKERS

Temporary employees, student assistants, or volunteers are the standard resources for move personnel. When funds are available to employ temporary help, use job placement services to screen and identify people. Contact employment agencies that specialize in temporary staffing. Some temporary workers will accept jobs only during a defined period of time or when the proposed schedule fits a personal timetable and will leave when a better offer or other obligation comes along. However, each project will attract employees who are serious about doing the work. The library offers these individuals work, albeit short-term, and a chance to get a good reference for another position.

Government agency placement services are a good source because their fees are low or nonexistent. The service may already be in the library—for example, Job Junction—and so the forms and the employees are within easy reach. Investigate city, county, state, or federal programs offering low-cost temporary help. The Federal Comprehensive Employment Training Act, or CETA, used to be an excellent source of help. Some counties and cities offer summer youth programs which provide labor free of charge or below minimum wage, but be prepared to do all of the required paperwork for these government-funded program. When using people from a temporary job program, hire about 20 percent more workers than the estimated number needed because some of the workers will leave for full-time or other employment during the course of the project.

Prison inmates are possible temporary move workers. Many correctional institutions run work-release programs. The correctional institution selects personnel, arranges transportation, meals, and on-site supervision. Supervision must be clearly understood before the project begins. If the move is planned to take five days or less, inmate movers are an excellent workforce resource. The hours of the move will be determined by the schedule of the correctional institution. Inmate movers are often in excellent physical condition and cooperative, helpful workers.

STUDENT ASSISTANTS

Student assistants are an excellent source of temporary labor and are usually willing and able to do the type of lifting and hauling required to move a library. College and university students are usually reliable workers because they need the money and because they care about making the arrangement of the library into a better place to work and study.

Many institutions restrict the total number of hours each student may work during the semester, and some regulate the number of work-hours per week. As a result, more people will have to be trained and more paperwork completed because of the greater number of individuals needed to get the total work hours required. Nonacademic libraries located close to a college or university should investigate the potential labor pool available from the nearby academic instititution. Obtaining reliable labor will offset the possible costs of transportation to and from the college residences.

Occasionally, high-school students are available through special work-release programs. The student pool can also be increased by hiring students from more than one institution, even though coordinating the schedule can be a nightmare. Clubs and other organizations in colleges and high schools may provide assistance—often in exchange for support of the club in the form of publicity or meeting space.

Schedule students for at least a two-hour time block. The ideal situation is to have one person commit an entire day, or at least half a day, to to the work. Schedule several teams of students to work simultaneously. Each team should have a back-up person and at least one student assigned as a "go-for." Scheduling students so work can be done during normal business hours is difficult when classes are in session. Whenever possible, moving projects should be scheduled for completion prior to exam periods—a time that seriously impacts the availability of the students.

A core of students may be identified as team leaders and assigned line supervisory responsibilities. These students can be responsible to one staff member or to the project manager. The student-team leaders will need the same information at the daily briefings as the regular staff. On-site supervisors, whether students or volunteers, need to have the same amount of authority on the job as regular staff members. Supervisors will have to shift workers from task to task, act when someone is not doing his or her fair share, and recommend dismissal when appropriate.

When the "platoon system" is used and work teams of four to eight students are scheduled to report for work at varied times, repeat the briefings as each team arrives. Frequently, student schedules mandate a temporary revision in staff reporting times. With many different starting times, put the daily briefing information in writing and make sure a staff member and a back-up are assigned to meet with the student team leaders as soon as they are on-site. Briefings should be well-organized and concise since every minute spent in a briefing is time taken from the actual move.

Many students have never worked before. A letter of reference in the file, solicited or unsolicited, rewards good workers. Time to write this letter should be scheduled by the space planner as soon as the project has ended. The letter written at this time will be more pertinent and meaningful than one written a few months later.

VOLUNTEERS

The use of volunteers for a single project has its advantages and disadvantages. Those agreeing to a finite task are reliable and will usually see the task through. However, if the move is to take more than a couple of days, do not expect to retain more than a few of the original volunteers. Moving books is a boring task, involving a lot of time and effort, and is not likely to lead to a long-term commitment.

Before committing to a volunteer labor force to accomplish all or part of the project, check to see if use of volunteers is viable. Suppose a volunteer is injured during the move? Investigate the legal and insurance aspects of using volunteers on the project.

If a library already has a corps of volunteers, will these individuals be considered "staff" during the move? This decision will be influenced by the volunteers themselves. The "regulars" may not mind licking stamps or working at the circulation desk, but they may object to or be physically unable to move books. Generally, a new pool of volunteers will be needed specifically for the move.

Plan an extensive campaign to recruit the volunteers, recruiting at a time close to the actual start of the move. People who volunteer too far in advance may not be able to carry through. The techniques used to recruit volunteers often affect the job performance of the worker. One popular method is the competition. For example, classes are allowed to compete for "who can move the most books at one time." Academic fraternities and sororities, social clubs and informal groups also like to compete.

The rewards and prizes vary from appropriate liquid refreshments and a party to a scholarship or cash award. The organizations and individuals expect publicity for their efforts and recognition for the turnout. Competition works best when there are goals throughout the project. Awards for the number of volunteers, the number of collective hours, the number of items moved, or the best overall effort are powerful motivators.

If the move is to be accomplished using a competitive reward system, plan to spend a considerable amount of money repairing books. With a contest, participants are aware of the prizes and the potential publicity; the work that must still go on is often of secondary importance. A team trying to win first prize by moving the most books will not be worried about damage to the books. The competition works when each team assumes responsibility for the performance of its members as they shift the material.

An agreement with a service organization may be possible: the group contributes a set number of volunteer-hours to help with the move in exchange for a set amount of money contributed to the organization or to a designated charity. For example, an agreement could state that for every hour of volunteer work up to a certain amount, the library will contribute an agreed-to dollar amount to the Shriners, or the Lions Club, or the Chamber of Commerce.

Be sure to specify in the agreement that the volunteers are needed in three- or four-hour blocks. Scheduling workers can be problem in an hour-for-contribution agreement: over 50 people will be ready and eager to help between 10:00 a.m. and 11:00 on Saturday, only three between 9:00 a.m. and 10:00 a.m. or 11:00 a.m. and 12:00 p.m., and none for the rest of the day. A project relying on volunteers should not impose a commitment which eventually costs more in training, staff stress, and confusion than it would cost to move without the volunteers. The "costs" are more than monetary.

When using volunteers, allow for two or three times the number of people-hours needed to do the project. Schedule people to definite work shifts of no more than four hours duration and make sure a staff member is assigned to supervise each work shift. Volunteers have the highest attrition rate of any type of worker, especially when the project takes more than one day. If the hours for implementing the project are Monday through Friday between 8:00 a.m. and 5:00 p.m., the chances of obtaining a good volunteer pool are reduced, and the total number of hours scheduled may have to be increased even more.

The library has obligations to the volunteer. Information and direction must be provided, and records of number of hours worked will have to be maintained since some volunteer activities earn credit. Volunteers are busy people; many are involved in more than one project. When this is the case, individuals may have to leave early, come late, and so on. Designate a volunteer coordinator—a person responsible for keeping aware of the constant exceptions and excuses and gathering necessary forms and paperwork. The volunteer coordinator maintains the message board, directs poeple to facilities for hanging coats, sitting and resting, restrooms, and beverage facilities. The library project manager and the volunteer coordinator must maintain a high level of enthusiasm among the team members. This is a difficult task, particularly when the library is providing full services. If the library is closed, more options are available. To raise morale and speed the progress of the work, pipe in music and encourage conversations.

PREPARING THE WORKFORCE

The orientation of new members of the workforce to the library and library operations is essential before they begin work. Do this the first time they are in the library by conducting a general meeting. The orientation need not be extensive, but the workers do need to be able to view the tasks connected to the move in the perspective of overall library operations; they have no idea that the books will have to be kept in order, or that the order has any significance, or that materials are to be handled in a special way. For example, if the books have to dusted as part of the move process, the moving staff should understand that dusting insures preservation of the collection. Another task is flagging materials in need of repair or cataloging attention. Inform the people handling the books what the library is looking for and why. This is also a good way to get people to care about the materials as they are working.

Before any workers agree to work on the move, they should have an idea of the complexity of the project and the amount of effort needed for the move. If materials are moved using boxes, the boxes will be heavy. Can the prospective worker lift a box that weighs more than 50 pounds? Can he or she lift several in a row or lift them for an extended period of time? It is not unknown after the first day in a library move to discover only one or two workers able to continue the work. If, on the other hand, everyone is aware of the nature of the task and the expectations involved, the chances of completing the job in a timely manner are increased.

Carefully supervise any worker moving an expensive collection. Generally, there is no method of discipline for the recalcitrant volunteer; the paid worker can be dismissed. Some individuals may be unsuited to the work, or to the other people, or to the library.

Identify tasks within the overall project which can be assigned in a way that separates workers who cannot get along with other team members or who cannot perform a particular task.

PROFESSIONAL MOVERS

The moving method is not as difficult to determine when the work is going to be done by an outside moving firm. Unless otherwise stated in the specifications, the company awarded the contract determines the method of moving and provides the equipment and personnel. Some move specifications require that the personnel hired be students at a particular institution or that the books be moved using a certain type of box or truck. (See the sample specifications in the Appendixes.)

Professional moving companies specializing in library moves exist and have been used sucessfully in some situations. They have equipment designed to move large segments of books at one time and require less time for orientation.

Selection of a moving company may be an option for the library; sometimes the company awarded the contract is determined by an outside agency. A contract with the county, state, school system, or college may include all moving or relocations during the term of the contract. But even if the moving company is preselected, it is still wise for the space planner to draw up bid specifications for the move. During this compilation, estimate the time-frame for completing the project and the exact amount of materials to be shifted from point to point, including books, furniture and equipment. The specification process gives the planner an opportunity to list conditions of the move in writing.

A contract is, by definition, an agreement which obligates both parties—the company awarded the contract as well as the firm issuing the contract. The space planner is obligated to make sure all local requirements for the contractor are listed and performed as listed. She or he should also see that the bill is paid in a timely manner. The contract may call for partial payments at each phase of the move, but payments are processed only if the library representative signs and agrees the work has been done in a satisfactory manner.

Common contractual conditions include providing the workers with keys or building access, parking spaces, access to a telephone, the location of temporarily stored items, clean-up, and a place to smoke and eat. If it has been specified that the move is to take place "after hours," then the hours have to be spelled out; the contractor needs to know what "after hours" means before he or she bids on the job. As part of the bidding process, the individuals or companies bidding estimate the number of hours it will take to perform the move and investigate the site for any obstacles. This means that provision must be made for on-site inspections before the date of the bid opening. The prospective bidders should carry out the inspection during normal working hours. Library personnel should accompany all prospective bidders on the site tours for security reasons and to provide explanations as needed.

In an era of fiscal constraints, a contractor's estimate must be very close. When the bids are close and tight, the space planner is not going to be in a position to change the conditions after the contract is awarded. Alterations of the contract after the bid award will most likely incur additional charges to the library. Making the prospective contractors aware of all of the circumstances benefits the library in many ways. For instance, if a class is in session in a section of the library, the movers may not have access to the hall outside the classroom or to the area in the library where the class is meeting. The need to hold classes throughout the move should be spelled out in the specifications and the contractor shown the classroom location when the prebid visit is made.

Moving companies provide fast workers. The speed and well-developed system of the professional mover can catch the library staff flat-footed. The local staff and plant department have time to stop and deal with a special circumstance, but the outside mover will not. The mover has estimated the time and staff required to do the move, and the costs for the move increase each time the move stops.

When professional movers are used, the contract should require them to work when the library staff works. Do not let outside movers move a library without supervision by the library staff; the results can be fatal. The specific arrangements must be clearly understood before the move starts. If the library is open from 10:00 to 6:00 p.m. and those are the hours when security and staff are available, state this in the proposal. Differences in reporting times may come to light only after an attempt to schedule the work and may be the result of union contracts.

The person in charge of the project for the moving company, the library union representative, and the library project manager must reach an agreement about work hours. This means breaks and lunch hours, starting and quitting times will be coordinated. In the corporate special library, company security policy may require that the building be unoccupied during certain hours. Do not assume this policy can be modified.

When there is a time lag between issuing the specifications and the start of the job, recheck the work conditions before the start date. After a contract has been signed with the company, a job meeting should be scheduled a few days before work commences so that representatives from both contracting parties can meet and agree to terms and conditions for the work. The representatives from the library who attend this meeting should be the people responsible for the move, usually the space planner and the project manager, if they are two different people.

At this meeting, discuss security, as well as the ground rules of the library, the institution, and the contractor. The people who will be working together have the opportunity to become familiar with names, faces, and the lines of command. One of the participants should summarize the meeting in writing and send copies to all attendees, to the moving company, and to the library director. This summary can be significant if changes or questions arise later about how closely the parties' performance accords with the contractual agreement.

Once the movers start, they will be very careful to make sure the furniture is placed in the locations as indicated on the plans, and they will check with the library supervisor to see if the location is correct. They will want to know where to put each item as soon as they enter the door, since they do not have the time to try several different positions. The project manager must be on-site with the floor plan, ready to help. If it looks like something is going wrong with the furniture arrangement, the project manager has to be quick enough to suggest an acceptable alternative.

OPERATIONAL DETAILS

The fire marshall should be consulted after the layouts are completed and interim locations set up. The entire plan will have to be revised if the locations do not meet the fire code. Fire extinguishers of the correct type, which have been recently checked, will be needed at the interim sites and in locations on the final plan.

Purchase extra equipment: a few extra bolts and screwdrivers keep the project rolling. Find out if there is a readily available petty cash fund or if one must be established. Lack of a roll of tape, tube of glue, or some other minor item should not be permitted to delay the move.

A few other points to consider:

- Are the shelves dusty?
- Has provision been made to dust and clean the book stock and the cabinets and furnishings? If not, make sure this is done.
- What about books found during the move process that need rebinding, relabeling, that are brittle, or that have plates, author's signature, special binding? Will they be moved, set aside, have a bookmark inserted, or a record completed so they can be retrieved later?
- The telephone companies must be contacted and a firm date set to move and reconnect equipment.
- Does anyone know how to shut off the water fountains so they can be moved?
- Is there a back-up power source to keep the elevators in operation while the electricians work on new wiring?
- Are barriers or barricades needed to keep patrons out of the project site?

Asking and answering these questions before the move is started will ease the implementation of the space plan.

LIBRARY OPERATIONS
DURING THE MOVE

Will the library be open to the public during the project? If the entire staff is working on the move, who is going to maintain regular library operations? Will books circulate? Will videotapes circulate? How about availablity of meeting rooms? Will any reference services be provided? Can the library operate while the materials are in transit? If the library is closed, what is the definition of "closed"? For instance, will interlibrary loan continue? How will ordering, receiving and bill payment be handled?

Although some libraries cannot close or reduce services or hours during a move, others are able to redefine their hours and the scope of operations. If the reorganization is going to take place over a long period of time, regular operations, in some form or another, will have to continue during the project. Occasionally, only part of the library is affected, but this is an exception; far more frequently, every department of the library is affected in one way or another.

All moves share four common elements: noise, dirt, security problems, and altered traffic pattterns. These elements influence the scope and magnitude of services being provided during the move. The noise and dirt, although inevitable, can be kept to a minimum with the cooperation of the contractor or the people doing the move. However, to a "minimum" still means regular operations will continue in a noisy, messy, atmosphere.

Security can be a nightmare, especially if construction is taking place during the move. Movers are concerned about the safety of personnel and the protection of their equipment. Contractors are concerned about protecting tools and other construction materials, as well as keeping unauthorized personnel away from construction sites to reduce liability. Scissors, tape, markers, screwdrivers, and hammers are likely to disappear unless a conscious effort is made to keep track of them. Cooperation between the library space planner and the contractor will maximize security and safety of materials, equipment, and personnel.

Library staff will have to monitor public accessiblity to high-risk areas so that patrons are kept out of the path of workers. The easiest way to do this is to set up cordons and ropes so that patrons are kept clear of the changing traffic patterns. The planner will have to reach agreement with the contractors and subcontractors to arrange traffic flow for construction materials and workers.

Both the amount of time estimated to complete the space reorganization and the magnitude of the job determine what should be done about regular library services and operations. Evaluate the impact of each phase of the project on all services before making a final decision about the interim operations. Since the publicity program is designed to make sure staff in each unit are aware of the progression and estimated time-frame of each phase, regular operations can be adjusted accordingly. A department should develop an alternative plan in case the moving project delays regular work for longer than expected.

Since construction is subject to outside factors, it is not unusual for the start-up date or dates for the beginning of each phase to be pushed back, mandating emergency interim operations or continuation of alternate arrangements. These delays will also affect the date all or part of the library departments and collections are expected to relocate. Since the library offices and the collections are usually moved on separate dates, library staff may be in one location and the materials in another, with the patrons expecting full library services and unwilling to understand why the library may remain closed. When this occurs, emergency interim operation arrangements should help to ease this situation.

The personnel responsible for supervising the relocation determines the success of the plan. A common mistake in library space implementation, especially when it involves the relocation of offices, is to assign anyone who happens to come in the door to be the project manager. Because of the potential for bad feelings and uncertainty over the new configuration, it is best to select as project manager a library staff member not directly involved in day-to-day supervision of the area to be moved. This individual will be responsible for timing and scheduling the move and will try to keep things running smoothly. He or she will not be able to eliminate all problems, but will be able to make sure the right desk keys get transferred to the right offices.

PUBLIC SERVICES

An interim public services station should be set up before the move starts if any services to the public are to continue during the move. To establish the station, the space planner may have to negotiate with the departments in the parent organization external to the library for space, wiring, and phone lines. The location of the interim station is the first topic for negotiation, especially if the present physical location of the library cannot be used. Maximum visibility will enhance the success of the operation.

Since the interim station is a special, multi-service operation, staff members having a grasp of all aspects of regular library operations should be selected to work at it. The staff who work at this station have to be aware of the forms and requirements for all library operations, such as booking rooms, accepting interlibrary loan requests, locating and circulating videotapes, collecting fines, operating copy equipment, and providing reference service. One or two microcomputers with phone lines may be set up to do circulation, database searching, interlibrary loan, connect with electronic bulletin boards, and house interim operations records.

Communication software is available for most of the systems that often use dedicated terminals such as OCLC, Westlaw, and LEXIS. If the library circulation system is out of commission for the move, talk to the vendor or programmer about setting up an interim, self-contained microcomputer program to handle transactions on a temporary basis. If the vendor cannot supply a program, a simple database management system can be set up by knowledgable library staff who have used microcomputers and database programs successfully.

THE INTERIM SITE

After an estimate of the length of time the stations will be needed, the next step is to estimate the anticipated volume of operations, which can be derived from the regular circulation, reshelving, interlibrary loan and reference figures. Use figures from a time in the library calendar parallel to the time of the move in order to arrive at a realistic estimate. If the move is to take place during the summer, for example, examine reports and figures related to previous summer's activities. The tally for reshelving materials in all sections of the collection will also yield an antipated base activity level at the interim station. Since it indicates the number of volumes used in-house, combined with the circulation figures, it will show the amount of staff time devoted to the public.

Publicity about the move will increase public awareness of the library. Expect increased library activity as a result. People who have had materials out for some time will decide that now is the time to return them, and there is always the curiosity draw attendant on moves. Since the traffic and demand on other library services may also increase, the interim station will be busy.

During routine operations the circulation functions may be separated into different physical areas throughout the library and controlled by different rules and systems. When planning the interim circulation activities, consider the tasks performed for each of these different circulation functions because policies should be merged as much as possible. For example, circulation of videotapes and CD's requires different space allocation and security provisions than book circulation. Will playback units be provided for these formats? The reserve circulation system may have extra requirements; perhaps it uses a different computer from the usual book circulation system. Reserve involves extra security. What will happen during the project when the reserve materials and the furniture are boxed and moved? Will alternate security arrangements be possible, or will temporary arrangements suffice?

Operations at the interim site will be facilitated if the rules are simplified and made consistent for all materials. Since this location is intended as a temporary accommodation for patrons, it should not be expected to replicate all library services. New rules might help reinforce this fact with patrons and staff.

When the circulation desk regularly serves as a multi-function station, special provisions must be made at the interim desk for each of the functions. The wiring and supplies for special functions will have to be added and may include special electricity, phone lines, and security. Regular office supplies are needed as well.

Reshelving: Reshelving will be centered around the interim site since this is the holding area for materials being returned to the collection. During the move, shelvers will have a difficult time shelving books when certain call-number areas are in transit. Establish a special temporary holding area because the shelver cannot put all the materials back in the "proper place" when portions of the collection are being moved. The project manager can determine, within a close time frame, which materials or units will be out of commission, and how long and what size the holding area should be, by extrapolating percentages of call-number ranges based on the distribution of the total daily circulation.

For example, assume that over 50 percent of an average day's circulation is fiction and that the fiction section of the collection is scheduled to be moved during an established block of time—a full day. If the library circulates an average of 500 items during the course of a day, and half of the circulation is fiction, then room in the holding area is needed for at least 250 items or books while the fiction materials are moved. If 25 percent of the circulation is in the 600 classification, the holding area needs to house 125 volumes in the 600s during each day the 600s are being moved. In the same library, if the fiction collection is to be boxed, stored, and shifted, more room will have to be allowed for the temporary storage of fiction until the collection is in its new location because of the anticipated number of fiction books off the shelves when the collection is boxed.

When the whole collection is to be shifted using booktrucks and the library has no more space, the holding concept is more difficult and more essential. In the case of the internal shift, the same trucks needed for reshelving will also be needed for the shift. When identifying the trucks to be part of the holding area, the library space planner will have to reduce the number of trucks committed to the move. The easiest thing to do is to divide the resources and commit some trucks to the move, some to the interim service point, and clearly mark both. The trucks should be divided before the final move timing is determined.

How will the routine shelving be accomplished? If the staff is to work on the move and do the regular library duties, then restrict the hours during which each function occurs. Assigning staff members to shelve for an hour or two before the move segment of the day starts may solve the problem.

Paging: The primary function of the interim site may be to page materials from the collection. If the materials are to paged, who will do the paging and how will it be accomplished? Will certain members of the staff become pages? Will paging be done "on demand"? Who will take the requests when the page is retrieving other materials? What about the times when the page is on a break? How can materials be paged in and out of a transient collection? What about the books in the sealed boxes? What about paging of materials off of the shelves and in the process of being moved? Guidelines and schedules for retrieval should be set up and announced in the publicity.

NONPRINT COLLECTIONS
The role that nonprint media play in the library and those departments that service and circulate the nonprint materials must be considered. Will only regularly circulating materials be retrieved for patrons? If so, should users be notified that the nonprint materials will not be available for duration of the project, or at least for the period when access to the library is through the interim circulation point? Will the videotape collection be inaccessible during the move? What about the software collection and the public-access microcomputers?

A decision must be made about location and access to indexes and databases on CD-ROM. If they are to be available, then the space and wiring to use them must be at the interim site and part of the interim setup should include set up and testing CD-ROM. Will these items be available at the interim site? If they are not, will emergency access be provided?

It is possible to arrange to lend microform readers, particularly if heavy users of film or fiche can be identified. It may be possible to "loan" a reader to an academic department for the duration of a move, or to a law office or other central location where one or more heavy users has access to the machines and the film or fiche. If the decision has been made not to circulate film and fiche or the material will be inaccessible during the move, another decision will have to made about articles needed on a "rush-emergency" basis. Will copies be provided, and if so, who will do it? The wisest decision may be to add a microform printer and supplies to the collection of equipment at the temporary site.

REFERENCE SERVICES

A section of the interim site should be committed to reference services. But will it be possible to provide reference services and keep patrons out of the path of the move? It won't be easy for the reference staff to answer questions at one location when the collection is at a second location and the contents of offices are at a third.

Offering limited telephone reference service with prearranged referrals may be the only answer or, as a partial solution, a ready-reference truck of books with a cordless telephone as a semi-mobile reference service point.

If reference services are not going to be offered during the move, or if the interim offering is limited, arrangements should be made to refer patrons to another library that has agreed to serve as a referral library. This information should appear in the publicity and be available at the interim site.

OTHER SERVICES

Photocopy machines are needed for print materials, particularly reference or noncirculating items. Paper and other supplies for the copy machine should be stocked at the interim site. The electrical requirements of these machines should be included in any preliminary listing of the requirements of the interim site.

What should be done with current newspapers and journals? Generally, every bit of space available at a temporary station is needed for running the station and circulating material. The relative importance of on-site use of newspapers and journals must be viewed in relation to the total library operation and the space available during the move. It may be possible to keep one or two popular newspapers or journals at the interim site, but only if there is nearby space for patrons to sit and read them. This requirement alone is often enough to eliminate the concept of housing newspapers at the interim site.

TECHNICAL SERVICES

Even though there are few, if any, concerns about mandatory patron access to the technical services area, the department's ability to operate affects all of the service areas in the library. For example, if the department handling the book orders does not have electricity during the heavy book-ordering period, the collection and remainder of the library's services will suffer. Searching will be halted and no orders can go out.

Obviously, if the technical services department depends on automated processing, processing will cease when the system is not operational. Electricity, telephones, and possibly air conditioning are minimal requirements for an automated system. If the move generates a lengthy delay before the relocated system is in place and operating, temporarily reassign staff to one or more aspects of the move operation as opposed to reverting to manual processing.

Increasing backlogs require accessible space. Interim locations will be needed if the move operations are expected to interrupt technical services for more than two weeks. The shelflist, terminals, acquisitions files, and professional tools must stay with the workers. If the delay is to be for a month or more, full wiring will be required for these temporary work stations.

Technical services support is required when moving the collection, since this department provides the finding tools to the library collections. Some routine processing will have to be delayed when the project requires changing labels on materials and changing library records, unless extra staff are hired. The magnitude of the record changes varies. If the decision was to use storage, and the item level record is to contain a note with entries in the public catalogs for patron information, then it is the responsibility of technical services to change the records. If location symbols are changed due to an alternative shelving technique, or if cards are changed to show new locations, or if space is to be regained by weeding, the change will not work without appropriate record changes.

Occasionally, a global change in an online system will resolve the record-changing workload. When this can be done, be sure to allow time and resources to back up the system before and immediately after the change. The backup process in this instance should include archival copies before and after the change.

MAIL

Make arrangements to store mail when the technical services

department and the kardexes or record-keeping files are inacessible. The project manager can work with the plant department or the custodial staff to insure that adequate, *secure* storage space for mail is available. The storage space for the mail should be in a location where items can be retrieved in an emergency. Set aside large boxes, clearly marked, for the incoming mail.

Serials and periodicals arriving on a regular basis must be checked in, dated, and some invoices processed for payment. If the record-keeping files are inaccessible, provision must be made to date the bunches of incoming material. Special mail-opening times should be built into each day's schedule, with a staff member assigned responsiblity for it. At a minimum, sort mail each day into two dated boxes—one for periodicals and newspapers and the other for "regular" correspondence. If facilities are available for additional sorting and storing, sort correspondence by department, bundle it, and date each bundle. Once the new mail room or offices are set up, the bundles can be delivered.

The labels for the mail should be different from the labels for the materials being moved and should be exceptionally bright and easy to notice. In the case of a completed library move, boxes or bags used to pack files and records must also be labeled differently from the mail. A stack of mail is easily lost in the confusion, and considerable time could pass before it is found.

NEW SERVICES

If the new space plan has been designed for the introduction of a new service, make sure all public service functions are set up so the staff have a chance to work though the new procedures and routines before they are offered to patrons. Delay the official announcement and introduction of the new service to give the staff a chance to feel comfortable with the configuration. Operate in an interim or trial mode so staff can troubleshoot and examine the service carefully before final policies and procedures are adopted. The troubleshooting time should be considered part of the moving process; it will show how the new service will either replace or fit into existing procedures.

A new service in a library that is not adding space generates a loss of space in some other area of the library. During the process of trading space, more than one function will have to be rearranged. This domino effect usually changes the work flow, affects morale, and modifies work techniques. New job descriptions will be needed and new ways to serve patrons devised. In this case, operating during the move provides an opportunity to test the space configuration before it is impossible or expensive to change.

NEW WORK STATIONS

The introduction of change in the workplace has been discussed at length in the business and personnel management literature.[1,2] Realigning offices and moving work stations is a significant change for everyone involved. The library space planner needs to be aware of resistance to the new design, equipment, office layout, or service and should consider activities to ease adjustment to the change. The staff may or may not voice their reactions. Sometimes reactions are so extreme that people resign. When moving around offices and redesigning the organization's structure, notice whether—even though the long-range goal may be commendable—the short-range product is flawed.

The space planner and the library administration will have decided before the shift starts if the relocation will be accomplished by moving the people or by moving the desks and the people with them. Each is a different form of implementing change. Each causes disruptions in the workflow and operations. Staff should participate in the project, especially those whose work stations are involved. Have the staff pack their own desks, mementos, and shelves.

IMPACT ON AREA LIBRARIES

Most libraries exist in a community of libraries. Changes in operations by any one of these libraries have an impact on the other libraries. When the only library in the area open on weekends must pull all staff to complete a move, thereby closing the library on weekends, the other libraries should be informed. If one library is going to be out of service for a period of time, consider formalizing cooperation by referring patrons to another library. In fact, the contact desk may be located in a neighboring library instead of the alternate or interim location in the same library or building. The interlibrary loan aspects of public services will, of course, be taken care of in the publicity phase of the project implementation. However, accurate information should also be given to the participating libraries. If two libraries have been working closely, all press releases should be distributed to the other library.

RESUMING OPERATIONS

When the interim locations and operations are no longer required, disassembly should be as well organized as assembly. Planning to move the equipment into the new or relocated sites should be done methodically, with attention to interruptions in operations and services during the move. Do not start operations and/or functions in the new locations until all records, equipment, and materials from the interim location have been removed. Allow at least one "settling in" day after the move or renovation is completed before a service or function is removed from the interim location. Expect some "down" time while the interim station is moved. If the project is running behind schedule, extend arrangements to use the borrowed resources that constitute the interim site.

REFERENCES

1. Rensis Likert, *The Human Organization: Its Management and Value* (New York: McGraw-Hill, 1967). Although dated, this basic text is well worth consulting.

William Ouchi, *Theory Z: How American Business Can Meet The Japanese Challenge* (Reading, Mass.: Addison Wesley, 1979). A classic that suggests ways to change traditional American approaches to management.

Thomas J. Peters and Robert H. Waterman, Jr., *In Search of Excellence: Lessons from America's Best-Run Companies*, (New York: Warner Books, 1984). A popular treatment of effective management of change.

Paul Hersey and Kenneth H. Blanchard, *Management of Organizational Behavior: Utilizing Human Resources*, 5th Edition (Englewood Cliffs, N.J.: Prentice-Hall, 1988). Another excellent resource.

2. Richard Steers and Lyman Porter, *Motivation and Work Behavior* (New York: McGraw-Hill, 1975). One of the best works in the area of employee motivation.

Frederick Herzberg, "One More Time: How Do You Motivate Employees?" *Harvard Business Review*, 65 (September/October 1987): 109-20.

Another classic, Herzberg contends that job enrichment is the key to motivating employees.

James O'Toole, "Employee Practices at the Best Managed Companies" *California Management Review*, 28 (Fall 1985): 35-67. Employee involvement and a sense of well-being are evident in the 'best managed' companies.

John R. Schermerhorn, Jr., "Team Development for High Performance Management" *Training & Development Journal*, 40 (November 1986): 38-41. A team development approach.

Cecil G. Miskel, "Motivation in Education Organizations" *Educational Administration Quarterly*, 18 (Summer 1982): 65-88. Summarizes three approaches to work motivation and six current motivational theories.

Dana C. Rooks, *Motivating Today's Library Staff* (Phoenix, Ariz.: Oryx Press, 1987). The last two citations are directed to the nonprofit sector.

9 MOVING AND WRAP-UP

Moving a library is like painting a room. Preliminary work is necessary before starting, and if done properly, the job goes smoothly. Once all the planning is completed and the project is set up, getting the move actually started and doing the work is anticlimactic. Everything falls into place because it has been planned down to the most minute step. Again, as in painting a room, this is the point where the quality of planning is tested. However, all the planning and preparation will only help ease what is basically an exhausting, dirty job.

BUT, BEFORE STARTING . . .

Before packing the first box or loading the first booktruck, we thought that the retelling of some war stories—of what has gone wrong in some library moves—would be enlightening. The locations have been changed and the names omitted, but the authors or colleagues have been involved in each of these situations.

Many stories involve contractors, subcontractors, and contract deadlines. Accurate, detailed bid specifications facilitate negotiations with contractors. However, contractors and subcontractors are often at the mercy of suppliers. If the $10,000 or $15,000 shelving order for a small library arrives at the factory at the same time as a very large order, there is a good chance the small order will be delayed.

At Library A, a battle occcured among the various contractors. The shelving supplier had subcontracted the shelving installation, and other bidders objected to the bid award. The library was ready to move, although the shelving was not installed. An outside mover had been given a firm start date, and since the library move was scheduled during a particularly busy time for the mover, delay was not possible. The staff had to cope with stacks of boxed shelving, and stacks of cartons containing the collection in the new location, until the shelf installer caught up to the move schedule. The mover charged extra money for additional cartons because books were not removed from cartons so that they could be reused.

Library B, upon moving into a new building, found that the heating and air-conditioning contractors had missed the deadlines; systems were not ready to go into operation until a few weeks after the move. Although the new building was sealed, with all air circulation and temperature dependent on the not-yet-operational systems, the staff still had to move the materials by a certain date because an outside mover had been contracted and the dates could not be changed. The library staff were assigned to supervise the move and had to work in the new location. The air in the library was unhealthy, and the staff used sick days, especially when the weather was poor. The move took longer than anticipated, thus delaying the opening of the library.

Library C had to move before the carpeting was delivered and installed. As a result, the shelves were installed contrary to the original plan, which called for placing stacks on the carpet. When the carpeting arrived, it had to be installed around the stacks. The stack area is now permanently defined by the carpet.

Library D closed for renovation and was ready to reopen with the new furnishings and equipment in place after a major rehabilitation involving installation of a new HVAC system, new lighting, construction of a new entry way, and construction or replacement of walls, ceilings, and floors. Only one thing kept the library from reopening: the book collection was missing. The library board had contracted with a firm to pack and store the collection for a certain amount of money. When the contractor was advised to return and unpack the books in the newly renovated building, the contractor insisted upon payment of additional monies, four times the amount set forth in the contract. The board pursued legal action.

Library E had to move before shelf-reading was conducted and after an active circulation period. It was almost impossible to move materials in order; the move took longer than planned; and the entire library staff had to be pressed into service to do a shelf-reading project at the new location.

Other libraries have inaccurately defined the staffing requirements for the move and ended up with more outside staff than needed and no one to supervise. Library F lost very valuable materials when temporary staff with time on their hands stole library materials, which they then tried to sell. Underestimated staffing requirements can be just as damaging. Library G's move took twice as long as planned because it did not have enough staff: over 60 percent of the moving crew found excuses not come back after working one-half day. Library H was forced to change the method of moving half way through the project because of a balky elevator, doubling the cost of the move.

When Library I used student assistants to move, training sessions and formal instructions were not offered, even though the entire collection was to be shifted, filling two-thirds of each new shelf. At the end of the move, when all of the money for extra staff had been expended, the project director discovered that, while all of the shelves were in order, the empty space was on the left side of the shelves, not on the right side. For some time after the project, shelvers were shifting books back to the left side as a regular part of their duties.

One large library numbered the card catalog sections in the wrong direction, and the movers placed the sections as numbered. To this day, users must go from right to left to use the catalog. Stories abound about card catalogs facing a new direction or staff having to shift all of the drawers in the unit as a result of not checking details during the planning phase of the move or the speed of professional movers outpacing available supervisors. In one move, vertical file cabinets were moved and placed in a line, but out of order. A complete rearrangement of the drawers and their contents was required but not possible because of the different cabinet manufacturers. The contents of the drawers had to be rearranged.

One planner lined up all of the desks in the new centralized support-staff section with the legs and typing stacks placed so that none of the electric typewriters could be plugged in. Work had to be delayed until the furniture was shifted so that the desks could fit properly.

And then there are the stories about the competitive moves. When one moving team got ahead of another during a "hot" competition, it was found that the team in the new location was ignoring the floor plan. About 10,000 volumes were shelved before the project manager discovered four full booktrucks.

The people stories are also fascinating. During Library J's move, the workers seemed to disappear every Friday at noon. They were going to a nearby race track, feeling they had worked hard enough all week to be entitled to the afternoon off. As a result, schedules had to be reordered because the workers could not be replaced and were not subject to discipline. In addition, since they had signed contracts for the "duration of the move," the workers wanted to extend the period of employment; and they were accomplishing this by working four and one half days per week.

In another move, a temporary worker refused to allow anyone near him as he believed he could lift the entire range of sections and move it as needed. This delayed the move for an hour until help arrived. Another temporary worker liked the library so much she hid at closing time. Security found her in her new "residence" at 5:00 a.m.

During another move, a student employee failed to understand the reasons for backshifting, even after repeated explanations; by the end of the morning, the entire backshift crew was grumbling.

The student was sent to work on another part of the project after lunch, and by midafternoon the backshift crew was once again in good spirits.

And then there are the stories about the problems caused when a piece of equipment disintegrated; or the weight load was underestimated and a ramp collapsed; or the shelving that arrived happened to have either all right or left sides and was the wrong color and depth; or the elevators broke down; or the right dollies were not available. . . .

STARTING THE MOVE

When the teams and the supervisors begin their work, unanticipated problems arise that mandate a change in the move process. Occasionally, the changes are brought about for an apparently silly reason—the tape for labeling boxes will not stick or the boxes are so marked up after a few uses, that a new labeling method must be created; the motorized lift truck used to transport booktrucks breaks down or runs out of gas; the volunteers drop out; the weather intervenes. The project manager must become adept at improvising on the spot. One move was delayed because no one could think of a way to get the specially designed bins through a doorway until the project manager removed the molding around the door.

As soon as the first step of the reorganization begins, start the publicity, establish interim operations, and have the moving crews in place if volunteers or locally supervised workers are to used. Crews are usually eager to start, so assign shelf-reading until the move has gotten into full swing for those crews who will have a lag until the cycle of the move is underway.

At the first meeting with the moving crew, explain what is being done, the mission of the library, and how the move fits into the overall priorities of the library and the organization. If this is done well, there might be a lower probablity of a crew member dropping a full box of books since all will be aware of the library's goals for preserving materials.

Explain each assignment and include in the explanation exactly what each team will be doing. If one team operates the elevator and another takes the materials off the shelves, then each team must understand the concept of the chain of events. During the course of a move, the teams may become competitive, creating backlogs.

This can be avoided if the teams understand that their tasks are part of an integrated whole and not part of a competition, by switching team assignments after each break, and by cross-training the teams.

Follow the first crew meeting with immediate action. The cycle will begin as the shelves are emptied, the containers are filled and stacked, and the first load of books transferred. Allocate enough time for the first three loads to go through all segments of the chain, then break for coffee. On the first day, the crews may not understand why a break is necessary and want to work through it. Do not allow this. Take the break and use the time to talk to the workers and encourage team spirit. Establish that the coffee breaks will indeed be for only 15 minutes and will take place in a certain location.

All of the locations in the move cycle should have materials or containers on site. Clocks in all of the locations should show the same time. If the operation stops in one location, operations should stop at all other locations as well. All stops in work must be synchronized to avoid losing valuable work time. Lack of close coordination costs lost hours further down the line and few projects have so much money as to be able to absorb them.

CONTINUING

After the first break, the move should begin to operate on its own rhythm and the value and validity of the schedule, and project timing for the operation will become apparent. Request comments from the moving crew at the end of the first day. They may offer suggestions for better ways of doing things. After meeting with the entire crew, during which everyone is complimented on their efforts, the supervisors and library staff should meet with the project manager to accept additional suggestions for smoothing out procedures and to discuss the appropriateness of the individual assignments of the crews.

By having the teams work on one assigned task during the first day, procedures for the operation will be ironed out. The second day of the move should involve cross-training. Teams can train each other on the tasks they performed the day before. The best time to cross-train is after the lunch break, since productivity often levels off during this period. Varying the assignments and the operations of the individual crew members maintains a higher productivity level. Because of cross-training at this point, jobs can be reassigned on the third day. A corps of trained workers is now available in case of absenteeism.

If the library staff are moving the stacks, do not try to move whole ranges of brace-frame shelving intact; they have to be dismantled and reassembled. This step should have been included in the timetable and the planning. When it is necessary to take the shelves apart, the components may become damaged, causing extra time to be spent on repair. In the collection-housing inventory, the potential for problems was noted and this is the point where the problems can slow the progress of the move.

Are replacement parts on order? Have they arrived? If so, shelving can be constructed in time to lock into the cycle of the move. When shelving diasssembly and assembly is underway, designate a "go-fer"—someone who will get the screwdriver, the needed shelving pieces, the hammer, and so forth—so the moving crews are not chasing all over the building looking for tools. In fact, the best way to assure a good work flow and prevent too much idle time is by having enough equipment and moving items on hand to take care of potential problems. Since wheels may fall off booktrucks or the trucks may break and be out of service for the move, a couple of trucks should be identified as spare or backup right from the beginning.

Label the shelves on the booktrucks at the start of the move so they are in consecutive order. Labeling trucks with magic marker is one option since it goes on quickly and stays visible for the duration of the move. However, the booktrucks are then permanently labled. Tape is another option, but it usally leaves a mark on the trucks and wears off during a move. Masking tape works best because it can be marked and it comes off easily. When it does wear off, teams should be alerted to replace it immediately.

Number the trucks consecutively, starting at the top of one side with shelf number one, then moving down, labeling the following shelves two, three, and then to the other side of the truck starting again at the top. The shelves should be numbered even if they do not hold the exact amount of materials needed to fill a shelf at the new location. Numbering speeds loading and unloading. If shifting or collection rearrangement is needed, the shifting should be done at the point where the materials are unloaded, not at the packing point.

Make a provision to cover the books if loaded booktrucks go outside during the move; otherwise, rain or snow will temporarily halt the project. An inexpensive way to cover the trucks is to use large plastic garbage bags, with the side seams torn out. These bags might not last for more than a few trips, but they will keep the move going despite bad weather. Be sure to have enough bags to cover each truck involved in the move.

When scheduling the teams, make sure two individuals are at each point where bumps, sharp corners, ramps, or other interruptions to moving the booktrucks are located. Getting on and off elevators, over door-jambs, over areas where carpeting begins and ends are trouble spots and places where the materials on the trucks can spill off. When the move involves loading booktrucks onto a truck, assign a crew to load and line up the booktrucks. A crew member should remain on the truck, reshelving items as they fall off during the ride. The booktrucks will fit loosely in most pickup trucks used for hauling. See if cinderblocks are available to put against the sides, serving as stops.

Try not to use anything other than a freight dolly to shift a stack of boxes containing books. The weight of several full boxes will be more than most library equipment can handle. Boxes can be labeled consecutively with different colors for each load, sub-collection, or call-number area. Number the boxes as the books are removed from the shelves. A given number of boxes can constitute a load and be labeled that way. A load may contain ten boxes or 60 or 600. The number moved at one time will, of course, depend on the type of conveyance used.

Do not leave the truck or the moving dolly filled to capacity at the end of the day unless the boxes are clearly marked with consecutive numbers and call-number sequences. Do not get in a situation where the boxes are moved to the new location, then stacked in front of the shelves where they are to be reshelved. Rarely is there enough room in the aisles for the boxes, and the shelves could be filled in the time it takes to arrange the boxes in front of the sections. Stack the boxes in reverse order outside of the sections so the top box is removed first. Labels should be removed or erased once the boxes are unpacked so they can be reused immmediately.

Make certain trash containers are available at each end of the move. Disintegrated labels and boxes and other miscellaneous debris will accumulate and should be disposed of promptly.

Extra copies of the proposed collection arrangement should be available at the new location. The project manager should re-check placement and call-number sequences after the move has been in process through a couple of cycles. If long runs of a call number such as a legal case law series or bound periodicals are to be moved, then identifying the shelf where each long run should start will help speed placment. When non-library personnel are putting material on the shelves, any step to simplify and reinforce will be worth the extra effort.

STOPPING

At least one-half hour before the end of the work day, make sure enough of the containers are full so that work is at each of the stations for the next morning's start-up. Also make sure that empty containers are available so the shelving crew can begin to fill them in the morning. If there are empty trucks to be returned or empty boxes to be stacked, leave them where the crew that checks boxes for damage and returns boxes to the loading point can work on the boxes. Closely coordinate quitting time among teams for security as well as work flow. It usually is not possible to leave full trucks in the elevator, but they can be placed just inside the door of the library so they can be loaded and transported the next day. If using a pickup truck or van that locks, then leave it full, locked, and ready to roll the next day. The entire activity is much like starting and stopping a production line; work needs to be at the stations at the first bell in the morning and after the breaks.

Lunchtime can be interpreted as a complete stop of the line. Another option is to stagger the lunch hours and continue activities with half a crew. Each has its disadvantage. The latter option means that the line will be at half strength for an extended period of time. But the first option requires all things to be locked in place so that the entire crew can take a lunch break.

SETTING UP OFFICES

The project for moving offices or setting up new services should also start with a meeting of the crew. Prepare and distribute handouts which include the new layout, a description of events, the progression of the move, and the office layout. The meeting should cover the same topics as the first crew meeting for a collection move: the objective of the project, the objectives the library, and how this particular project will fit into the overall scheme of the operation. The mover and the work crews should clearly understand the layout: what scale has been used and what the symbols represent.

Most office moves are completed by professional movers or the maintenance department or crews. Although a crew meeting is not held, multiple copies of layouts are available and library personnel who know exactly where each item is to be placed to the last detail are on site. If cords or wires are to dropped behind furniture, this should be done as part of the move before the item is permanently in place.

SECURITY DURING THE MOVE

Whether the movers are outside movers or regular library employees, they are probably already covered by insurance. However, bonding companies can provide low-cost employee insurance against theft for a finite period of time. If a lot of material is to be moved, this option should be investigated. Some time after a major school district moved books and equipment to storage, one of the staff members happened to walk past a pawn shop and discovered why the district had apparently retrieved space: many of the portable materials had made it to a new location—the pawn shop, which was displaying in its window two l6mm film projectors, identity tags and all; the shopowner was convinced it was surplus.

SECURITY

Security should be addressed in written documentation and be an assigned responsiblity of supervisors and every person working with the project. One security technique is requiring workers to sign statements affirming that they are aware of the value of the collection and are committed to preserving it. Discuss security at the first crew meeting and mention it at every subsequent meeting. Since troughs, booktrucks, and unsealed boxes are open-ended, they can encourage theft. Part of the task of the line supervisor is to prevent theft and vandalism. When a special collection or archival collection is moved, employ extra security staff. During breaks, have a special security person watch the materials. Seal boxes and count items before and after each phase of the operation. Volunteers or inmate movers can be directed to exit through the library security gate.

During the first phase of the operation, the space planner should conduct a well-publicized security investigation. One way to check security is to mark several books and then check the progess of the books through the line. Security should involve spot checks of coats and parcels, as well as random investigation of boxes or booktrucks. Check to see that all of the materials are indeed going where intended. Microcomputers, microform readers, and desk calculators are high-risk items because they are portable and can be sold. Equipment can be checked using the numbers and information from the furnishings and equipment assessment.

MISCALCULATIONS

The space planner may face the consequences of miscalculations and will have to improvise to meet the changes in plans. Changes should be made immediately, on site, as opposed to reshifting later. When the work appears to be going too slowly, identify the obstacles causing the slowdown and see if they can be corrected. Do not panic and try to move things in a way that might be faster but less orderly or require an additional step. Remember, the move was planned to be not only the fastest way to get things done, but also the best way, taking into consideration the budget, the materials, and the staff. Careful planning goes out the window if major changes are made mid-project without good reason. The information in the space data file will be useful for responding to emergencies and should be consulted before initiating action. It will contain dimensions of equipment and furnishings, as well as details about the space the collection consumes.

When moves are going faster than anticipated, be grateful and use the workers in another capacity when and if the move is completed ahead of schedule. Perhaps the crew can make range-finders or conduct a final shelf-reading before the stacks are opened or the compact shelving is ready to use. Do not assume a move be will completed ahead of schedule simply because the initial pace is rapid.

DEBRIEFING

Post-move meetings with moving crews and the library staff are held to gather as much information as possible. These meetings should be held at the end of the last working day. Actually, since the teams will finish work at different times, the final debriefing is most effective if held with each crew as it completes its final tasks.

This meeting is not a social activity. The movers should report to the project manager about the condition of the library and suggest changes in procedures for future moves. People who are involved with the move and the new arrangement of the library can provide valuable input about traffic flow, collection condition, lighting, and other problems before they have an impact on operations.

Since library staff members have been used as supervisors, they should be able to provide the administration with information on potential problems and help plan details of the next phase of the reorganization. Add anecdotal notes and staff input to the space data file in a "relocation" section of the file. Their concerns can be addressed before the library begins to operate at full strength with the new configuration and/or service.

WRAP-UP

After the move, have the crew put away or otherwise dispose of all of the materials used to do the moving. The booktrucks and troughs have to be allocated throughout the library and the boxes distributed or burned. Make a final check of shelves for bookends and incomplete tasks. Do this before all of the extra workers are gone and there is no more energy for the project.

A post-project meeting with the entire library workforce should be held after a trial period with the new configuration—perhaps in two weeks. It takes at least this long for the staff to adjust their work styles to the physical changes. Find out how the new arrangement is working. This meeting will provide an opportunity to air concerns and to restate the fact that the change is not temporary. The often-negative initial response to new locations is frequently a reaction to the change itself rather than to whether things are actually better or worse. The post-project discussion, therefore, should focus on real, not perceived, problems or gripes.

REVISING THE SPACE DATA FILE

By definition, the space data file is intended to serve as a resource for decision making and, as such, is a guide for change. The problems and unexpected occurrences which are part and parcel of moving projects and reorganizations also dictate changes in the space data file. While the move is in process, the planner should keep notes for use after project's completion, when additional revisions are made in the file.

Layouts, photographs, and floor plans gathered for one project are resources for the next. Because of this, they should be made a permanent part of the space data file. Take photographs of the new space once everything is in place and label and date everything. Because of the rearrangement, staff collections and services will use different space than listed in the file.

The project is now complete and the library has come full circle. Events throughout the project and suggestions received at the debriefing have resulted in concrete directions for future use of the space. The planner should update the space data file, reflecting the suggestions and the changes which have been made, and issue a final project report. Keeping the raw data current provides a base of information for responding to future space planning needs. Each library reorganization is part of a space utilization continuum. Services and needs change; technological changes frequently dictate mini-space revisions. In fact, a full-blown space planning project, undertaken without time pressure, can easily generate space not suited to the equipment it is intended to house by the time the project is completed. While flexibility is expensive, the basis for the inevitable changes is built into the space data file as the project is completed.

APPENDIX

STANDARD BID SPECIFICATIONS

The standard boiler-plate language and routine forms placed at the beginning of bid specifications will be available from, or dictated by, agencies and/or regulations external to the library. Boiler-plate language is part of all bid specifications released by an agency and usually includes noncollusive bidding certification, bonding requirements, as well as general instructions to bidders and information about where and how to submit bids.

Bid specifications from other libraries are a valuable resource for format and depth of specifications. Review more than one example, if possible. Sample documents from the same geographic region or political subdivision as the library will contain the specifications to meet local requirements.

Each set of specifications should include the following:

1. Inventory, in linear footage, of collections to be moved.
2. Inventory of furnishing to be moved: office equipment, shelving, machinery, supply cabinets, microform cabinets.
3. Instructions for packing and unpacking; and special handling instructions.
4. Instructions for removing, moving, and reinstalling equipment; list of equipment.
5. Start and end dates; hours of operations; date beyond which the contract will be invalid. Must a library staff member be present when movers are working?
6. List of equipment and supplies provided by the bidder; supplies and equipment provided by the library.
7. Previous library moving experience requirements; requirements for names and addresses of contact persons from previous library moves.
8. Outline of required information about supervisors provided by the contractor; resumés or personnel information about the move personnel.
9. Special strictures: Site for temporary storage? Limited access to freight elevators? Can the loading dock accommodate only trucks of a certain height? Should all new staff be hired from one institution? Are special passes required at gates? No smoking/eating/drinking in library except in designated area?
10. Special security requirements.

11. Post-move clean-up requirements and responsibilities for the site; disposal of the materials used during the move.
12. Hours, days, and locations when the collections and furnishings may be surveyed by prospective bidders.
13. Insurance requirements relating to the personnel, equipment, and building.
14. Contact person for the library or organization, including full name, address, telephone numbers, and hours of availability.

SAMPLE BID

DETAILED SPECIFICATIONS FOR MOVING LIBRARY COLLECTIONS, FURNISHINGS, AND EQUIPMENT FOR _____ LIBRARY

Scope

The Contractor shall perform all services and furnish supervision, labor, and all equipment and supplies required to remove the property from *present locations,* transport it to *new locations,* and place the property in the *new locations* as directed by the authorized employees of the Library.

The property to be moved consists of the library collections and equipment, including but not limited to books, bound periodicals, unbound periodicals, microfilm, pamphlets, newspapers, phonograph records, framed prints, files, office furniture, office machines, typewriters, duplicating machines, microcomputers, microfilm readers, microform cabinets, shelving, supplies, and other materials.

Metal shelving specified by the Library will be dismantled, moved and reassembled including cross ties, and bolted to the floor by the Contractor in the locations specified by authorized Library staff.

Qualifications of Bidders

The contract will be awarded to a mover who demonstrated experience in moving libraries. The Bidder is required to submit, as references, a list of all library moves completed during the last five years. The Bidder must also include the names and address of persons to be contracted at the previous institutions.

Prior to the contract award, the Bidder will submit the resumés of persons who will serve as supervisors for the contractor during the move. These resumés will contain full information about participation in library moves and a detailed listing of prior supervisory experience.

Prior to the contract award, the Bidder will submit a statement of the numbers and types of equipment owned by said Bidder which will be used in this move, and a statement of additional equipment which will be required for the move. A separate statement must be included listing the number and type of mobile moving carts owned by the Bidder that will be used to move the collections and the number of additional carts required for this move which the Bidder will purchase. The bid will not be awarded until the successful Bidder has submitted a satisfactory plan for the move, detailing the handling of all problem areas. This plan must be approved by the Library Director or his/her designee.

To warrant consideration, the Bidder must have demonstrated to the complete satisfaction of the (Board of Trustees) (School Board) (Regents) (Library Board) that he or she is fully aware of all factors involved in the move and can schedule his or her staff and equipment to accomplish the move within the specified time. Some of these factors are:

- thorough inspection and understanding of all physical facilities involved with the move
- Understanding of the nature of the materials, the proper sequence for books, and timing of the move to insure a smoothly integrated correct placement of collections in the new building.

Special Instructions

The Contractor will furnish supervision, all labor, mobile moving cards, trucking, hand trucks, dollies with rubber wheels, and all other materials necessary for the move.

- All furniture and equipment will be removed and relocated as designated by tags or labels provided by the Contractor, indicating floor number, area number, and attached to each item to be moved.
- Materials are to be packed in closed containers and sealed at the point of packing.
- All work will be done under the overall supervision of Library staff during the normal work day. Specific hours of the work day, including breaks, will be defined by the Library Project Manager and the Contractor's supervisor.

The collections will be packed, labeled, moved, unpacked and placed in designated locations as specified by the Library. All materials are the reshelved in their existing order according to instructions from the Library Project Manager. Instructions will be provided prior to moving any group of materials. The Contractor's supervisory staff will be expected to be familiar with the (Library of Congress) (Dewey) Classification System and shelve according to it.

Included with this notice is an approximate inventory of the materials, equipment, and furnishings to be moved. However, the actual material to be moved, the physical locations of the materials, and the problems of accessing the materials may be ascertained by a physical inspection at the premises where materials and furnishings are presently located.

At the present location the Contractor shall have unrestricted use of the freight elevator and one other elevator to be designated by the (Library) (School) (College).

The Contractor will be responsible for protecting from damage any elevators, hallways, floors, stairways, windows, and window sills used in the move. Carpeting must have protective covering during the move. The Contractor must protect all surfaces in the library. The building must not be damaged in any way.

The Contractor shall promptly remove from the premises all debris, materials, and equipment resulting from the work of this contract.

The Contractor, at his or her own expense, shall obtain and maintain all necessary permits, franchises, licenses or other authorities required for lawfully effecting the movements, handling, and other services to be performed under this contract.

The successful Bidder will be required to pay the minimum hourly rates established by the (New York State Industrial Commissioner in accordance with Section 220, Subdivision 3, and Section 220-d of the Labor Law.)

All materials, equipment, machines, supplies, etcetera, will be moved under security measures approved by the Library's representative.

The (Board of Trustees) (School Board) (Regents) (Library Board) reserve the right to stop the services under the contract at any time upon determination of that Body that the contractor is unable or incapable of performing the service in such a manner as it may deem advisable. If the costs of completing the work exceed the amount of the contract, the Contractor and his surety shall be liable for all excess costs.

Schedules

The schedule is to be worked out between the Contractor and the Library in the best interests of the most efficient moving operation.

All equipment and materials to be moved may be surveyed only on _____ between the hours of _____ in (building) (room). Bids will be accepted only from firms who have surveyed the site.

Arrangements may be made to inspect the premises through the Library Contact _____, Office Number _____, Telephone _____ between the hours of _____am and _____pm, Monday through Friday.

The move shall commence beginning _____. The move is to be completed in (fourteen) consecutive working days between _____ and _____. In no case will it extend beyond (fourteen) consecutive working days from the start date.

Said schedule and beginning dates may be delayed subject to building readiness. Prompt notice will be given in the event of delay.

Requirements

The successful Bidder agrees to comply with and does hereby agree to accept the following conditions:

- Each Bidder must inform himself or herself by personal examination of specifications and locations of the proposed services and such other means as he or she may select of the character, quality and extent of service to be performed and the conditions under which the work is to be executed including a definite understanding of all requirements relating to building facilities, elevator service, and such other services as may be required in all buildings connected with the moving operation.
- The (Board of Trustees) (School Board) (Regents) (Library Board) will make no allowance or concession to a bidder for any alleged misunderstanding or misinformation relating to quantity, character, location, or extent of service to be performed, or other conditions.
- The bid price shall cover the cost of furnishing all services, materials, and equipment required or the proper and efficient conduct of the move, to the satisfaction of the organizational representatives, in strict accordance with the specification and pursuant to the contract.
- All equipment used for moving purposes shall be subject to the approval of the Library. The Library reserves the right to deny the use of any equipment for performance of the contract that may cause damage to the buildings or facilities.
- If any Library-owned or Library-controlled property is lost or damaged during the performance of the contract, the Contractor shall be responsible and pay the full amount of such loss of damage. The property amount will be assessed by a third party, hired by the Library. For materials damaged or lost from the collections, the Library shall determine the current market value. The third party appraisal will be done at the Contractor's expense.
- The Contractor, in company with a representative of the Library, shall inspect all property prior to the start of the move to satisfy her/himself as to its condition and at the same time shall record any existing damage, which must be certified by the Library/Director designee.

Payment

Following the successful completion of (one-fourth, one-half) of the move, the Contractor will receive _____ percent of money, with the final amount payable in full at successful completion.

SAMPLE BID SHEET

(*Name of company*) proposes to furnish all services, including supervision and labor, and all equipment and supplies required in moving the present (Library) (collection) to the new (building) (location) in accordance with specifications furnished by _____. A representative of (*name of company*), (*name of employee*), inspected the premises on _____ in compliance with the bid specifications.

1. Pack, label, transport, unpack, and reshelve approximately _____ volumes of books and approximately _____ periodicals and newspapers. Move _____ atlas cases, map cases, and _____ microform cabinets and the collections associated with each.
2. Dismantle, move, resassemble, and bolt to the floor (where directed) approximately _____ linear feet of shelving.
3. Move and set in place office furniture, office equipment, media equipment and other equipment and supplies.

ONE TOTAL BID FOR ALL ITEMS $_____

Name of company _____

By _____ Title _____

Street _____

City, State, Zipcode _____

Phone number (area code) _____

Date _____

INVENTORY LIST

This sample inventory list illustrates the variety and diversity of the items to be included in moving a library. The list should be organized by room and/or location and include the following items and the quantity of each item:

Aquariums
Atlas stands
Bicycle racks
Bookcases—dimensions, number of shelves, wooden or metal
Booktrucks
Bulletin Boards—attached, composition
CRT's and peripherals
Card Catalogs—sizes, number of cases, type of unit
Carrels
Cash Register
Chairs by type—side chairs, secretarial chairs, lounge chairs, arm chairs
Clocks
Coat racks
Contents of storage closets
Desks by type—single pedestal, double pedestal, returns
Display cases and materials
Display racks
Electronic security system
Ergonomic workstations
File cabinets—list number of drawers: legal size, letter size
Lockers—book lockers or coat lockers
Map cases
Microform equipment
Microform and AV cabinets
Microwave ovens
Pencil sharpeners
Photocopiers and supplies
Plants
Portable equipment—screens, podium
Refrigerators
Shelving—by type, function and amount
Sidetables
Sofas
Supplies
Supply cabinets—size
Tables—by size
Wastebaskets
Wet carrels

BASIC RESOURCES

A SPACE PLANNER'S READING SHELF

A selected list of basic readings and resources;if the Bibliography *appears overwhelming, these sources are a good starting point for those beginning a space planning project.*

"Library Buildings," *Library Trends* (Fall 1987, Volume 26, Issue 2) edited by Anders C. Dahlgren, contains articles on design trends in public, school, special and academic library buildings, and articles on lighting, mechanical systems, environmental design, staff furnishings, and alternatives to the construction of a new library.

"Planning aids for new library buildings," *Illinois Libraries*, (November 1985, Volume 67, Issue 9: 794-810) by HBW Associates, Inc. This article succinctly covers building design and planning from A-Z and has a brief and very useful bibliography.

Planning Academic and Research Library Buildings by Philip D. Leighton and David C. Weber (Chicago: American Library Association, 1986). A space planning classic and although geared toward academic libraries, every space planner would do well to have a copy of this work and to consult it frequently.

"Space management for libraries" by Dale S. Montanelli in *Illinois Libraries* (February 1987, Volume 69, Issue 2: 130-138) is an overview of starting the space management process and what is involved in the process.

Richard Boss' book *Information Technologies and Space Planning for Libraries and Information Centers* (Boston: G. K. Hall, 1987) is a good place to start when preparing for new and emerging technologies and their applications in libraries. The chapter on existing space planning formulas may be of special assistance in justifying the need for additional space.

The Winter 1987 issue of *Library Hi Tech* (Issue 20, Volume 5, Number 4) is primarily devoted to building design and new technologies. It contains "The Forgiving Building: A Library Building Consultants' Symposium on the Design, Construction, and Remodeling of Libraries to Support a High-Tech Future."

Electronic Spreadsheets for Libraries by Lawrence W. S. Auld (Phoenix: Oryx Press, 1986) contains a chapter "Estimating Shelving Capacity." Three different spreadsheet applications are presented: Shelving Capacity Variables compares shelving capacity for up to five different arrangements; Predicting Shelving Capacity for projecting capacities of up to five areas; and Shelving Density by Shelf, Section, Range, and Total details a shelf-by-shelf snapshot of ranges, illustratiing the amount of empty space remaining.

Library Journal puts together an "Architectural Issue" each December, listing new libraries, additions, renovations, and projects in process. For each project, cost, square footage, funding source and and architect are listed.

The June 1987 issue of *Library Administration & Management* (Volume 1, Number 3) is devoted to buildings. Articles on floor loading, compact shelving specifications, architect-client relationships, plus "Planning Expanded Facilities: Issues for Small Public Libraries" and "Analyzing Architectural and Interior Design" make this particularly helpful.

Planning Library Buildings: From Decision to Design, edited by Lester K. Smith, (Chicago: American Library Association, LAMA, BES 1986) reports the proceedings of a 1984 preconference sponsored by the Building and Equipment Section of the Library Administration and Management Association. Some of the papers included are on building programs, planning teams, building consultants, needs assessment, role and selection of the architect, schematic design, contract documents, and drawings.

"Library Design: What not to do" by Robert H. Rohlf *American Libraries* (February 1986, Volume 17, Issue 2: 100-104). The title says it all.

The Building and Equipment Section of LAMA produces the "Building Consultants List."

BIBLIOGRAPHY

GENERAL

American Association of School Librarians and Association for Education Communications and Technology. *Information Power: Guidelines for School Library Media Programs*. (Chicago: ALA, 1988).

Anderson, Marvin Roger and Emily J. Batista, "Space Requirement Checklist for Basic Resources" *Legal Reference Services Quarterly,* Spring 1984; 4 (1): 65-71.

Bedenbaugh, Edna, "Facility Planning in the School Media Center" *Indiana Media Journal,* Summer 1987; 9 (4): 3-4.

Buckingham, Betty Jo, *Plan for Progress in the Library/Learning Resource Center . . . Area Schools. Guidelines for Development of Library/Learning Resource Centers in Iowa's Area Schools* (Des Moines: Iowa State Department of Education, 1987): ED 287 485.

Clay, Edwin S. and Gailyn Hlavka, "Does this building work?" *Library Administration and Management,* June 1987, 1 (3): 105-6.

Cohen, Elaine, "Analyzing Architectural and Interior Design" *Library Administration and Management,* June 1987; 1 (3): 91-2.

Cohen, Elaine and Aaron Cohen, *Designing and Space Planning for Libraries: A Behavioral Guide* (New York: R. R. Bowker, 1979).

Conrow, Jane, "Remodeling large academic libraries: Survival hints" *College and Research Libraries,* December 1985; 46 (11): 600-04.

Crystal Lake Public Library, "Ready, willing and able: preparing the staff team" *Illinois Libraries,* November 1985; 67 (9): 786-91.

Dahlgren, Anders C., "An alternative to library building standards" *Illinois Libraries,* November 1985; 67 (9): 772-7.

Dahlgren, Anders C., Issue Editor, "Library Buildings" *Library Trends,* Fall 1987; 36 (2).

Dahlgren, Anders C., *Planning the Small Public Library Building* (Chicago: American Library Association, 1985). Note: Small Libraries Publications No. 11.

Dahlgren, Anders C., "Planning Expanded Facilities: Issues for Small Public Libraries" *Library Administration and Management,* June 1987; 1 (3): 80-4.

Ellsworth, Ralph E., "ABC's of Remodeling/Enlarging an Academic Library Building: A Personal Statement" *Journal of Academic Librarianship,* January 1982; 7: 333-43.

Ellsworth, Ralph E., *Planning the College and University Library Building: A Book for Campus Planners and Architects* (Boulder, Colo.: Pruett Press, 1968).

Faulkner-Brown, H., (United Kingdom). Section: Library Buildings and Equipment. Papers. *IFLA General Conference, 1986. Management and Technology Division:* "Changes in Library Buildings". The Hague (Netherlands): International Federation of Library Associations and Institutions; 1986; ED 280 492.

Gore, Daniel, Editor, *Farewell to Alexandria: Solutions to Space, Growth, and Performance Problems of Libraries.* (Westport, Conn.: Greenwood Press, 1976).

Grossman, George S., "Programming for the New Library: An Overview" *Law Library Journal,* Summer 1987; 79 (3): 489-98.

Hall, Richard B., "Library Space Utilization Methodology" *Library Journal,* June 1979; 103: 2379-2383.

Hannigan, Jane A., "Charette: Media Facilities Design" *School Media Quarterly,* Spring 1974; 2 (3): 185-294.

Haymond, Jay "Adaptive Reuse of Old Buildings for Archives" *American Archivist,* Winter 1982; 45: 11-18.

HBW Associates, Inc., "Planning aids for new library buildings" *Illinois Libraries,* November 1985; 67 (9): 794-810.

Irvine, Betty Jo, *Slide Libraries: A Guide for Academic Institutions, Museums, and Special Collections* (Littleton, Colo.: Libraries Unlimited, 1979).

Kaser, David, "Academic Library Buildings: Their Evolution and Prospects" *Advances in Library Administration and Organization* (Greenwich, Conn.: JAI Press, Inc., 1988) 7: 149-60.

Kurtz, Winifred M., "Changes, Changes" *Illinois Libraries,* January 1988; 70 (1): 19-21.

Langmead, Stephen and Margaret Beckman, *New Library Design: Guidelines to Planning Academic Library Buildings* (New York: John Wiley and Sons, 1970).

Larason, Larry and Rebecca Dicario, *Personal Space and User Preference for Patterns of Carrel Arrangement in an Academic Library,* 1982: ED 222 166. Note: Paper presented at the annual convention of the American Library Association.

Larsgaard, Mary Lynette, *Map Librarianship: An Introduction.* Second Edition (Littleton, Colo.: Libraries Unlimited, 1987).

Leighton, Philip D. and David C. Weber, *Planning Academic and Research Library Buildings* (Chicago: American Library Association, 1986).

Lieberfeld, Lawrence, "The Curious Case of the Library Building" *College and Research Libraries,* July 1983; 44 (4): 277-82.

Lushington, Nolan and Willis N. Mills, Jr., *Libraries Designed for Users: A planning handbook* (Hamden, Conn.: Library Professional Publications, 1980).

Martin, Jess A., "Planning the New NIH Research Library" *Special Libraries,* January 1968; 59: 30-38.

Mason, Ellsworth, *Mason on Library Buildings* (Metuchen, N.J.: Scarecrow Press, 1980).

Metz, T. John, "What works—what doesn't" *American Libraries,* February 1987; 18 (2): 110-15.

Miller, Rosanna, "The Map Collection, Arizona State University Libraries" *Information Bulletin* (Western Association of Map Libraries), March 1987; 18 (2): 149-156.

Montanelli, Dale S., "Space management for libraries" *Illinois Libraries,* February 1987; 69 (2): 130-38.

Mount, Ellis, Issue Editor, "Innovations in Planning Facilities for Sci-Tech Libraries" *Science & Technology Libraries,* Fall 1986; 7 (1).

Novak, Gloria, "Building Planning in Austerity" *Austerity Management in Academic Libraries.* John F. Harvey and Peter Spyers-Duran, Editors (Metuchen, N.J.: The Scarecrow Press, 1984): 185-204.

Office of Management Studies, *Building Renovation in ARL Libraries* (Washington, D.C. : Association of Research Libraries, September 1983). Note: Spec flyer 97.

Pinzelik, Barbara P., "Rearranging Occupied Space" *Collection Management,* Spring/Summer 1983; 5 (1/2): 89-1-3.

Planning Barrier-free Libraries: A Guide for Renovation and Construction of Libraries Serving Blind and Physically Handicapped Readers (Washington, D.C.: National Library Service for the Blind and Physically Handicapped, Library of Congress, 1981).

Rohlf, Robert H., "Library Design: what not to do" *American Libraries,* February 1986; 17 (2): 100-104.

Rohlf, Robert H., "New Factor in Planning Public Library Buildings" *Public Libraries,* Summer 1987; 26: 52-53.

Schwartz, Mortimer, "Building Planning for a New Law School Library" *Law Library Journal,* May 1968; 61 (2): 73-87.

Smith, Lester K., *Planning Library Buildings: From Decision to Design,* June 1984 (Dallas, Tex./Chicago: Building and Equipment Section, LAMA, ALA, 1986).

Thompson, Godfrey, *Planning and Design of Library Buildings,* Second edition (New York: Nichols Publishing Co., 1977).

SPACE PLANNING FOR NEW TECHNOLOGIES

Boss, Richard W., *Information Technologies and Space Planning for Libraries and Information Centers* (Boston: G. K. Hall, 1987).

Brownrigg, Edwin B., "Library Automation: Building and Equipment Considerations in Implementing Computer Technology" *Advances in*

Library Administration and Organization (Greenwich, Conn.: JAI Press, Inc., 1982): 43-53. Note: Volume 1.

Cohen, Elaine and Aaron Cohen, *Automation, Space Management, and Productivity: A Guide for Libraries* (New York: R. R. Bowker Company, 1982).

Downing, Jeff and June Koelker, "Infomart: Intelligent Design, Intelligent Use" *Library Hi Tech,* Winter 1987; 5 (4): 77-99. Note: Issue 20.

Drabenstott, Jon, "The Consultants' and Vendors' Corner: Designing Library Facilities for a High Tech Future" *Library Hi Tech,* Winter 1987; 5 (4): 103-111. Note: Issue 20.

Fuhlrott, Rolf, "The Impact of Technology on Library Buildings" *Advances in Library Administration and Organization* (Greenwich, Conn.: JAI Press, Inc., 1985): 133-157. Note: Volume 4.

Garten, Edward D., "Conceptualizing Library Office Functions as Preparation for an Automated Environment" *Advances in Library Administration and Management* (Greenwich, Conn.: JAI Press, Inc., 1986): 173-195. Note: Volume 6.

Hudson, Kathy, "Historic Buildings and Modern Technology: The California State Library Remodels for Automation—A Case Study" *Library Hi Tech,* Winter 19875; 5 (4): 49-58. Note: Issue 20.

"Information Technology and Space Planning" *Library Systems Newsletter,* November 1985; V (11): 81-83.

Lamkin, Bernice, "A Media Center for the 21st Century" *School Library Journal,* November 1986; 33 (3): 25-29.

Lancaster, F. W., *Libraries and Librarians in an Age of Electronics* (Arlington, Va.: Information Resources Press, 1982).

Michaels, David Leroy, "Technology's Impact on Library Interior Planning" *Library Hi Tech,* Winter 1987; 5 (4): 59-63. Note: Issue 20.

Novak, Gloria, Editor, "The Forgiving Building: A Library Building Consultants' Symposium on the Design, Construction, and Remodeling of Libraries to Support a High-Tech Future" *Library Hi Tech,* Winter 1987; 5 (4): 77-99. Note: Issue 20.

Paskoff, Beth M., Editor, "Contemporary Technology in Libraries" *Library Trends,* Winter 1989; 37 (3).

Price, Bennett, "Computer Power: Part 1, Distribution of Power (and Communications)" *Library Hi Tech,* 1988; 6 (4): 91-100. Note: Issue 24.

Rouse, Roscoe, Jr., "Whiter the Book? Considerations for Library Planning in the Age of Electronics" *Advances in Library Administration and Organization* (Greenwich, Conn.: JAI Press Inc.; 1985): 159-175. Note: Volume 4.

USING COMPUTER PROGRAMS FOR SPACE PLANNING

Auld, Lawrence W. S., *Electronic Spreadsheets for Libraries.* (Phoenix: Oryx Press, 1986).

Carlson, Barbara A., "Using Lotus 1-2-3 to Shift and Maintain a Serials Collection" *The Serials Librarian,* December 1987; 13 (4): 39-58.

Ellis, Judith Compton, "Planning and executing a major bookshift/move using an electronic spreadsheet" *College & Research Libraries News,* May 1988; 5: 282-7.

Simon, Rose, "Computer Tells Books Where to Go: A BASIC Program for Shifting Collections" *North Carolina Libraries,* Spring 1987; 45 (1): 36-37.

Watkins, Steven G., "Space Planning and Collection Analysis with Enable" *Library Software Review,* November-December 1987; 6 (6): 367-368.

SELECTING AND WORKING WITH CONSULTANTS AND ARCHITECTS

Beckman, Margaret, "The Library Building Consultant and the Library Planning Team". Smith, Lester K., editor. *Planning Library Buildings: From Decision to Design,* June 1984; Dallas, Tex./Chicago: Library Administration and Management Association, American Library Association; 1986: 57-67.

Heimsath, C., "How to talk to the Architect" *Texas Library Journal,* Winter 1977; 53: 21-23.

Lushington, Nolan, *Consultants and Library Boards* (Chicago: American Library Trustee Association, 1981, 6-page leaflet). (ALTA Publication; No. 2).

McAdams, Nancy R., "The Role and Selection of the Architect" Smith, Lester K., editor. *Planning Library Buildings: From Decision to Design,* June 1984; Dallas, Tex./Chicago: Library Administration and Management Association, American Library Association; 1986: 107-18.

Rohlf, Robert H., "The Selection of An Architect" *Public Libraries,* Spring 1982; 21 (1): 5-8.

Rohlfing, Kenneth, "An Architect's Perspective" *Law Library Journal,* Summer 1987; 79 (3): 499-519.

Simon, Matthew J. and George Yourke, "Building a Solid Architect-Client Relationship" *Library Administration and Management,* June 1987; 1 (3): 100-104.

Vivrette, Lyndon and James A. Clark, "You Have No One to Blame But Yourself" *Community & Junior College Libraries;* Summer 1984, 2 (4): 5-12.

Zenke, Mary H., "Assembling Dreams and Reality: The Job of the Library Building Consultant" *Illinois Libraries,* November 1985; 67 (9): 792-794.

LIBRARY MOVES

Alley, Brian, "A Utility Book Truck Designed for Moving Library Collections" *Library Acquisitions: Theory and Practice,* 1979; 3: 33-7.

Amodeo, Anthony J., "Helpful Hints for Moving or Shifting Collections" *College and Research Libraries,* March 1983; 44: 83-8.

Ansell, E., "The Move of the Cambridge University Library" *Library Association Record,* March 1935; 2: 92-6.

Blaustein, Albert P. and Jessie L. Matthews, "Space for a Periodical Collection" *Law Library Journal,* May 1967; 60: 147-61.

Clifton, A., "Moving the Johannesburg Public Library's Serials and Newspaper Collection Into a New Stack" *South African Librarian,* July 1971; 39: 56-59.

Craigie, Anne L., "Moving Day" *Library Journal,* May 15, 1938; 63: 388-89.

Draper, Wesley, "Method of Transfer of Books for Safekeeping" *Medical Association Bulletin,* October 1942; 30: 457-460.

"Fast Response to Library Emergency" *College and Research Library News,* March 1980; 41: 57-58.

Gibson, D. B., "Planning and Executing a Library Move: The Experience of the Home Office Library" *State Librarian,* March 1978; 26: 9-10.

Hamilton, Patricia and Pam Hindman, "Moving a Public Library Collection" *Public Libraries,* Spring 1987; 26 (1); 4-7.

Head, Anita K., "Remodeling and Expanding Space: Library Services during the Construction Period" *Law Library Journal,* Summer 1987; 79 (3): 535-45. Note: Erratum, Volume 79 (4): 845.

Hoefler, Barbara Burton, "Mini Operation for a Maxi Move" *Hawaii Library Association Journal,* June 1971; 28: 24-26.

Ifidon, Sam E., "Moving an Academic Library" *Journal of Academic Librarianship,* January 1979; 4: 434-7.

Jesse, William H., "Moving Books" *Library Quarterly,* July 1941: 328-33.

Johnson, Nancy P., "Rearranging a Law Library: A Case Study" *Law Library Journal,* Winter 1980; 73: 132-3.

Jorgensen, William, "Rearranging a Book Collection" *Library Journal,* June 1941; 66: 570-1.

Josselyn, Lloyd W., "Moving the Enoch Pratt Library" *Library Journal,* June 1, 1933; 58: 480-82.

Kephart, John E., *Moving a Library.* Urbana-Champaign: University of Illinois Library School, 1951. Note: Occasional Papers, No. 21.

Kurkul, Donna Lee, "The Planning, Implementation and Movement of an Academic Library Collection" *College and Research Libraries,* July 1983; 44: 220-34.

Kurth, William H. and Ray W. Grim, *Moving a Library* (New York: Scarecrow Press, 1966).

"LC begins major book move, stack cleaning program" *LC Information Bulletin,* June 23, 1972; 31: 280-81.

Lumb, Audrey E., "Moving an Academic Library: A Case Study" *Journal of Librarianship,* October 1972; 4: 253-71.

Meinke, Darrel M., "Pulling the rug out from under the stacks (revisited)" *College & Research Libraries News,* May 1988; 49 (5): 288-289.

Metz, T. John, "Getting from Here to There: Keeping an Academic Library in Operation During Construction Renovation". *Advances in Library Administration and Organization.* Greenwich, Conn.: JAI Press, Inc.; 1986: 207-19. Note: Volume 5.

O'Connor, Grace, "Book brigade fills new public library". *Times-Union.* Albany, New York; January 27, 1989; Section B: 2.

Pascoe, J. D., "A Move of the National Archives". *New Zealand Libraries,* November 1966; 25: 195-9.

Roberts, Matt, "Some ideas on Moving a Book Collection". *College and Research Libraries,* March 1966; 27: 103-8.

Roth, Britain G., "Moving a Medical Center Library". *Special Libraries,* Winter 1985; 76 (1): 31-4.

Schick, Joan L., "Bagging Books Helps School Library Move". *U*N*A*B*A*S*H*E*D Librarian;* 1976; 21: 3-4.

Schunck, Russell J., "Librarian's Nightmare". *Library Journal;* October 1, 1941; 66: 817-821.

Segesta, James, "Pulling the rug out from under the stacks". *College & Research Libraries News;* July/August 1986; 47 (7): 441-444.

Seiler, Susan L. and Terri J. Robar, "Reference Service vs. Work Crews: Meeting the Needs of both during a Collection Shift". *The Reference Librarian;* 1987; 19: 327-339.

Sexton, Katheryn, "Moving into the New San Antonio Public Library". *Library Journal;* Summer 1968; 44: 69-70.

Sheetz, A. Coleman, "The Journey of the 360,000". *Pennsylvania Library and Museum Notes;* 13: 133-136.

Snyder, Nancy, "How to Move a 60,000 volume Public Library for $1,000 (or Enlist the National Guard)". *U*N*A*B*A*S*H*E*D Librarian;* 1976; 21: 3-4.

Spyers-Duran, Peter, *Moving Library Materials.* Milwaukee, Wisc.: Library Associates of UW-M; 1964.

Stebbins, Howard L., "Moving Day". *Wilson Library Bulletin;* May 1941; 15: 425.

Stokes, Katharine M. and Knoll, Margaret F., "Moving the Pennsylvania State College Library". *Wilson Library Bulletin;* November 1941; 16: 230-238.

"Students Pitch-in to Move Yakima School Library". *Library News Bulletin;* January 1968; 35: 36.

Townsend, Robert B., "Moving the Illinois State University Library". *Illinois Libraries;* April 1977; 59: 295-299.

Uzelac, Constance, "Moving a Fragmented Collection". *Special Libraries;* September 1969; 60: 457-458.

Von Ancken, Eve Elisabeth, "A Personal Account of Closing a School Library". *School Library Journal;* September 1980: 38-40.

Wilbur, Earl M., "Economy in Moving a Library". *Library Journal;* March 1, 1922; 47: 217.

Woodward, W. B., "Laughing All the Way to the Stack". *Library Association Record;* July 1977; 79: 365.

INDEX

Ruth A. Fraley is Director and Chief Law Librarian, Office of Libraries and Records Management, Office of Court Administration, of the State of New York Unified Court System, in Albany, New York.

Carol Lee Anderson is Assistant Director of Access Services for the University Libraries of the State University of New York at Albany.

Book design: Gloria Brown
Cover design: Gregory Apicella
Typography: Roberts/Churcher